HOW DARE YOU

Inspecting the Rhetorical Kill-shots of America's Most Banned Comedian, Owen Benjamin

JACOB TELLING

How Dare You
Copyright © 2020 by Jacob Telling

Tellwell Talent
www.tellwell.ca

ISBN
978-0-2288-3481-6 (Paperback)
978-0-2288-3482-3 (eBook)

One of my biggest accomplishments in my entire career was destroying "how dare you" as a mechanism of control.

Owen Benjamin #862, 11:12

Civil - ization: *secularly organized—the process of becoming*

(or)

Civilization: *The process of becoming secularly organized*

For all the "*how dare you*" people:
If you hadn't been such a nightmare,
the rest of us would still be asleep.
Maybe we can return the favor.

TABLE OF CONTENTS

PREFACE

In a digital sense, Owen Benjamin is a marked man. Answering the question of why isn't difficult. In mainstream cancel culture, where political correctness runs the show, an outspoken masculine giant tends to make enemies, especially when he's effective at convincing an audience. Combine such competence with controversy and you've got a whole world of "how dare yous" aimed your way. How dare a comedian say something contentious? They dare because it's their job. A comedian keeps his lights on by revealing truths that are too uncomfortable for people to say. They crack jokes to break tension. Great comedians say what others are secretly thinking, making sure to get a few laughs in the process. For his temperament, Owen has earned himself the nickname "Big Bear." With his size, protective instincts, and proclivity to roar, the title certainly fits: he is a man of great amplitude. Like a literal bear wandering the streets, anytime Owen comes to town things get interesting for their high stakes. The pattern that's emerged on social platforms has become endearing for its absurdity: Big Bear says a few outlandish things and finds himself kicked off yet another platform. Regardless of the irritation, it doesn't seem to matter how many times Big Bear gets pushed out of a magic matrix in the sky, he just lands back on his feet in reality, better grounded for the experience. Smell the roses, as they say. Twitter? Banned. Patreon? Banned. PayPal, YouTube, Facebook, Instagram? Banned.[1] With a mountain of Owen's digital heads piled up, it doesn't take a genius to see the pattern of targeted executions. Having a high IQ and speaking honestly does, however, clearly offend whatever backroom machinery is driving these enormous and powerful corporate tech engines we call companies.

Although Owen Benjamin's story of exactly how he's been kicked off of everything is an interesting one to tell, it's not the focus of this book. For the uninitiated, all

---

[1]   The list goes on.

they need to know about Owen Benjamin is that before becoming a successful (and controversial) livestreamer, he was an accomplished mainstream comic who got along with everyone. Owen was in movies and TV shows, he headlined, produced multiple specials, and achieved everything that an aspiring comedian could possibly hope for—including being painted on the wall of the Hollywood Improv. Owen Benjamin became "problematic" when he started pointing his finger at catastrophes in our culture. Predators don't like exposure.

Beyond the pragmatic side of comedy, there's something in the music of it that's inherently captivating to us; like any other form of art, the craft of professional comedy pulls us in. We are moved by the flair of dancing musical notes, thundering literary works, and gut-busting humor in a way that's difficult to explain. However, like anything inherently valuable, the same quality that creates a virtue also creates its vice; all it takes is a shift in context. What is big cannot also be small. What is smooth cannot also be rough. What is fluid cannot also be solid. The quality that gives Owen an authentic voice that resonates with people is the same one that gets him in trouble with these social media platforms. If a human being was to overlook the nature of enormous scale, it could seem pretty odd that such a competent provider of entertainment would be so heavily censored . . . on platforms of entertainment. Through a business lens, that picture looks inverted. Why would a corporation kill its best providers?

One perspective is that Owen is just a bad guy and that these companies were right to cut out the rot by kicking a comedian off social media for the unforgiveable crime of committing comedy. "His style is just barbaric," they say, "truly beneath the distinguished class and dignified prominence that is becoming of a proper modern comrade." Indeed, in the enlightened minds of the truly woke, Owen is just a "racist, bigot, homophobe," whose crass behavior is anything but beyond reproach. How dare you say, "Part of me wishes slavery would come back so Shaun King would admit he's white," or, "Until David Hogg grows some hair on his balls, he can't tell grown men how to live."[2] Ultimately, their argument boils down to something simple: If you commit thoughtcrime by speaking against the stated positions of modern progressivism, you should be severely punished. Comply or you're out.

If the debate seems too close to call, I'll bring the jury in and end the suspense. Down here on Earth, with our feet firmly planted in warm, soft grass next to a sturdy, happy home, we live in reality. Up is up, down is down, yes means yes, and no means no. Corporate boardrooms aren't exactly champions of moral ethos. At a large enough scale, no institution is. By optimizing for economic growth, these organizations ethically degenerate. Eventually the unfeeling math of the algorithm takes over the system,

---

[2]   If you're wondering what it takes to get kicked off Twitter, by the way, apparently that will do it.

incentivizing fallible people for the absolute worst in a moral race to the bottom. The heart of man is, and will always be, easily corruptible, forever hosting the fickle Solzhenitsyn line between good and evil.[3] Some people take the ticket and rise to the tops of some pretty psychotic hierarchies of money and power, where corruption breeds corruption. Others, at some point during their ascent, refuse the emperor and get cut out, leaving a void for someone more . . . cooperative. In his honorable stand against the horror of Hollywood pedophilia and child abuse, Owen ended up with naught but a message and a microphone in the woods to protect and provide for his family.

Such is the geometry of what's upside down. Throw Owen Benjamin's name in the google machine, and you'll find all sorts of spurious accusations,[4] countless articles, and videos that make every attempt to paint the man as some sort of repugnant scoundrel: alt-right this, Nazi that, bigot, homophobe, etc. What they lack in cleverness, or creativity, they make up for with dishonesty and persistence. Say "bad man" enough times and undiscerning people will believe it. Repetition is really

---

[3]   Solzhenitsyn famously pointed out how the line between good and evil is divided not across groups like political parties or businesses, but right through the heart of every individual living man or woman.

[4]   Unless you go to infogalactic.com.

all it takes. Amazingly, it doesn't seem to matter that the voice is coming through a screen. Men and women blindly trust the authority in their pocket, ignoring the reality that propagation without investigation is indoctrination.

It's all nonsense. Go to a show, and who do you find in the crowd? Angry little trolls? Ignorant overgrown brutes? Illiterate rejects of society? Not at all; it's the exact opposite. Owen's audience is some of the most kind, intelligent, funny, and well put-together people you'll ever meet. Despite the worst censorship an American influencer has ever experienced, loyal listeners of every kind and creed continue to amass in droves. Why are people so captivated by Owen's comedy? Why are they changing jobs, flipping their lifestyles, or writing books after listening to him speak? Because in contrast to the unbearable drivel coming out of the mainstream nonsense vampires, Owen is saying things that are authentically resonating with ordinary, honest people, a refreshing change from the unrelenting fear porn and indignant caterwauling coming out of the mainstream. Men to women, young to old, and sharp to dull, Big Bear's audience is strikingly immune to demographic pigeon-holing. He's breaking cognitive spells and helping living men and women find purpose where there was once only rage, confusion, and despair. Everyone is tired of having their life force sucked out of them. We're turning to something authentic.

Earning a loyal audience, however, has come with its costs. It's not all sunshine and gravy for the Big Bear. There's a certain kind of anarchy built into the space within which he resides. Being constantly ahead of the curve is a difficult place to be, as those who wish to remain stagnant are hostile to those who instigate change. At the leading edge of culture and ahead of the zeitgeist is the natural territory of a great comedian. Such vigorous terrain is filled with an erratic climate of clowns responding to a bullish enterprise that that just went full rodeo. This chaos demotes the prim and the proper, promoting instead the rashness and impulsivity of the eternally outspoken goof. Dangerously poking and precariously prodding, the court jester aims his punchy antics at the king. While a healthy society permits such candid jabs, a tyrannical state controller simply rules with an axe, cutting the comedy short with a steely and violent hatred for unruly, independent thought. While the online heads of our jesters roll, the autocratic minds of our corporate emperors are being revealed for their decision to swing the iron. Modern comedy has replaced punk rock; a more honest and revealing flavor of art is being broadcast from the stage.

As we'll see, this whole mechanism hinges on competing cultures: opposing systems of values that can't cooperate. Some people want to be civil and submit to control to better outsource discomfort and avoid conflict. Others want to be left alone to better maintain their challenging albeit honorable lives. Two cats in a bag. The values that Owen is advocating for have earned him the honor of social shame, stigma, and financial losses much to the delight of the men and women who would like to see honorable freedoms squashed into oblivion if it means more safety and comfort. For the desired directions of these two separate cultural hierarchies, the awkward tug-of-war wages. Unlike our adversaries, droves of humble men and women who simply aspire to have a happy family, purpose, and beauty in their lives want Owen—and representatives of traditional American ideals like him—to succeed.

This book is the first in a three-part series about Owen Benjamin that starts with culture, transitions to politics, and ends with some pretty jarring ideas. Such a trilogy is meant to get any reader up to speed on what the Big Bear has been roaring about for the last few thousand hours of livestreaming. My hope for *How Dare You* is that readers find this book to be both enjoyable and enlightening as I have found with Owen's livestream. Before we get going, it's also worth understanding the method to Owen's supposed madness—it's built right into his nickname. Big Bear is large, loud, and intimidating. Physically and mentally, he's a formidable man capable of every kind of leverage: an awesome quality in the right hands. Although he spends much of his time being a giant goofy teddy bear, he's also partial to roaring and breaking out the proverbial claws. Even if you're one of the types who doesn't like a masculine, aggressive style of comedy (which is my favorite kind of comedy), it's worth taking a quick look at the ideas that Owen has been working through at the very least. An entire grassroots counterculture has been developing and is now burgeoning into a jungle due to its vigor. For the people who don't like his style, learning what he has to say from a safe distance is still better than not at all; you don't have to risk upending your whole life to engage with these ideas on a live camera broadcast on the internet in front of millions like the Big Bear did. You could, however, take a few hours to try to understand why, by reading this book. After all, if a man is willing to sacrifice so much and fight so hard for just a few ideas, you can't help but wonder: What is he fighting for? What does Owen know that I don't?

This book is an efficient way to learn. *How Dare You* is set up to perform two functions: To distill some of Owen's best rhetoric from thousands of hours of his livestream/podcast audio into one accessible place for safekeeping, and to make a concentrated argument, in my own words, for some of the honorable values that he is advocating for.[5] If I'm successful, this will be a cathartic read for anyone that follows Owen and a great introduction to some foreign ideas for anyone that doesn't. If you liked it, go ahead and pass it on. What's tricky about this

---

[5]   I mean rhetoric in the technical sense of the word: persuasive phrases that use emotion rather than pure logic to argue a point. In common-parlance use of the term *rhetoric*, many people assume that the rhetorical speaker is lying or speaking with predatory intent. This certainly need not be the case. Rhetoric is a tool like any other: it can be used in whichever way the wielder chooses. Owen uses rhetoric in pursuit of convincing others to pursue honorable living.

book is that I'm quoting Owen, but I also can't claim to speak for him. To address this potential source of discrepancy, I'll just unapologetically write what I believe and hope for the best. I'll make every attempt to be honest and fair, but no attempt to hide my obvious bias: I like Owen Benjamin. I'm both a fan of his comedy and a loyal supporter of what he's doing. Although I doubt many people who see Owen as a pariah will read this book, I'll nonetheless offer an unsolicited piece of advice for any that do: Avoid running from information you don't like in a fit of ego and rage. It's childish. They're just ideas; you don't have to hate someone who disagrees with you as long as you know they're both honest and trying their best. Good people have compassion for their friends. Great people have compassion for their enemies. If you see yourself as being on the other team, you owe it to your soul to try to separate the truth from the tribe. Let the arguments—both rhetorically and dialectically—of your opponents speak for themselves. If you can truly understand where the other side is coming from, you'll be better off, even if you still don't agree. Long-term knowledge is worth short-term discomfort. Just be fair and make an honest attempt to see the validity of these arguments. What happens after that is up to you.

A note about quotes:

> I think there's more truth in tone than there is in words.

Episode #714

One of the challenges of this book has been the effective conversion of the spoken word into the written word; inevitably, something gets lost in translation. Learning to recognize which quotes work well written down and which ones resonate mostly for their tone or context has taken some trial and error. To this end, I'm still learning.

In the first iteration of this book, I assigned each paragraph its own quote. While I like that this method of splicing quotes directly into the text makes it clear that Big Bear and I are in a similar conceptual place on these issues, this strategy proved to break up the flow of the book itself. For the sake of continuity, the quotes have instead been concentrated at the back of each chapter in a separate addendum. The order in which the first bank of quotes shows up are a reflection of the paragraphs I have written and should serve as a summary of the chapter. I encourage readers to think back and internalize the arguments I've made as they read these quotes. Starting in chapter 2, partway through the addendum is a divide separating the quotes corresponding to individual paragraphs from quotes that advocate the value of the chapter more generally; these general quotes are presented in no particular order.

This next paragraph can be skipped by anyone who does not care about the context of the quote citations.

When I first started writing down quotes, I had no aspirations for creating a book with them, I just wrote down what resonated with me. Consequently, the majority of the quotes lacking any timestamp took place in the early days of Owen's streaming, around the 100–200 stream range. Thankfully, I started writing down timestamps early on, although my book project was not yet a conscious idea. The astute reader will notice that there aren't many quotes in this book that fall within the 300–600 stream range. Many of these quotes, for their subject matter, have been reserved for books two and three in the *How Dare You* trilogy. For the same content-matching reason, many of the quotes in this book are from the early stages of Owen's streaming and are thus missing their timestamp. Some quotes are missing timestamps because they were emailed in. Others, simply because I made a mistake.[6] Unfortunately, most of the early quotes that do have timestamps don't line up, and even if they did you'd probably have a tough time finding the video/podcast online until they're uploaded on Unauthorized.tv. This is because in the process of Owen getting banned everywhere, some numbers seem to have been jumbled up. While my instinct is to go back and provide you, dear reader, with a perfectly consistent, codified set of quote citations, the opportunity cost of doing so at this time doesn't seem worth it. Once all the streams are reliably available for readers to retroactively listen to all streams based on accurate timestamps on Unauthorized. tv, I'll consider releasing a revised version of this book with updated quotes, but don't hold your breath! For now we'll

---

[6]   Thanks to everyone who emailed me a quote or three!

just have to settle, humbly accepting that perfection is an enemy of the good. As such, many timestamps merely serve to provide a general sense of context in terms of timeline and have thus had their hours/minutes removed. The streams have undergone many changes in the way they have been codified over the years. Most streams labelled in the 900s or 1000s (in this text) were night streams, or bonus streams, that took place in the 700 range. Some streams are labeled with dates (these are "bonus streams"), while others are labeled with numbers (these are the "day streams"). In other words, the timestamps are a mess. My apologies. To circumvent this problem, the basic rule is this: If there is an hour/minute marker on a quote's timestamp, it means that the quote was already available on Unauthorized.tv and you are able to reliably go back and listen to it at the time of this writing. For the minority of people who would like to make the effort to verify the authenticity of earlier quotes, you'll either have to be patient and listen to whole streams if you can find them (which just sounds like a win-win), or simply trust that I've recorded Owen's words in a way that upholds my values: honestly.

CHAPTER 1

Values

What do you value? Have you ever stopped to really think about it? Every day you wake up and step out of bed to complete an odd series of benign tasks. Why? What's your purpose? Is it to make money? Do you even know what money is, or what you're trying to do with it? Is it for your family, and are you doing what is best for them? Have you taken a step back to look at the bigger picture? Where's the best place to live—the city? The suburbs? The country? What are your priorities? Are you resolutely pursuing knowledge? Who do you trust? Have you scrutinized your sources of information? What reason do you have to blindly believe the people who manufacture the lens through which you see the world? Everybody puts trust in something, or someone. Who in your life is assigned the burden of proof, and who gets the benefit of the doubt? Do you trust the black mirror in your pocket? What did they—or it—do to earn your valuable trust? Why do they get the honor of filling your head with their opinions? What do you spend your time thinking about? What matters to you? What's meaningful?

When I finally asked myself these tough questions, years ago, it felt awful, like the emotional equivalent of beating myself with a brick. Melodrama aside, this line of questioning was uncomfortable for the reality that it revealed: I hadn't thought through anything. I was passively existing: letting my decisions manifest on their own, lacking self-awareness, easily influenced by the ambitions of others. Unfortunately, this is common. It's a serious challenge to be judicious and answer imposing questions. Many don't even bother to try. Left to our own devices, it's by definition easiest to fall into the path of least resistance: listlessly coasting through this modern first-world life, accepting the offer of a culture that's both void of iron purpose and saturated with greasy indulgence. The typical city boy goes to college to extend out an infantilized youth, where he falls into heavy debt, learns nothing useful, and cements an addiction to pornography.

Talk about uninspiring. Unfortunately for the chronically comfortable, such ingredients compose a recipe for nihilistic disaster, a real Hell on Earth. Without a plumb, solid foundation to build your personal house of values upon, you risk the whole thing collapsing in on itself, internally eroded for the warped rot of deadly sins. Soft sheets won't save you from the nightmares of your own soft mind. You need to stand for something so you won't fall for anything. So again, what do you stand for? What are your guiding morals? Your principles? Your values?

I'll speak candidly: If you want to be a complete human being, you'll need a whole hierarchy of values to live an honorable life. Look behind the scenes of a business tycoon who will do anything for money, a celebrity who will do anything for fame, or a politician who will do anything for power, and you'll find a bizarrely horrifying existence. Assuming you don't want to get involved in the slave trade for fancier pants, chemically castrating your child to elevate your social status in Hollywood, or murder a few people for a velvet seat in public office, you're going to want to maintain a kind of balancing act between your different principles. Money isn't everything. Status isn't everything. Power isn't everything. A virtuous balance between a thriving family, a healthy body, and a strong mind with which to engage in your own free decisions is a much better goal to start with and build upon.

What makes this whole endeavor of being a principled person a challenge in the first place is the nature of competing values: it's not always clear when one value takes priority over another. Just like how you don't get to pick only one principle, you also don't get to pick them all. Every virtue needs a restraint to avoid becoming its own vice. These restraints come in the form of other virtues, keeping each other in line, competing in a hierarchy of priority. Opportunity costs are everywhere. Perhaps you've got an affluent and interesting career that both provides a good life for your family and engages you. That's a beautiful thing. Focus too much on work, though, and both you and your family will suffer. In another domain, perhaps you enjoy the benefits of being likable, but focus too much on social clout and you'll find yourself bending and twisting the truth until it becomes outright dishonest. Flip such a dichotomy and the problem persists. Perhaps you enjoy getting to the truth, but focus too much on it and you'll alienate everyone you know.

Each principle is a form of currency: one can be traded for another. But what's the exchange rate? How does the value of each denomination stack up? We can't come up with some magical formula for values. Some of the quirkier people out there might like to try, but the reality is that it's not going to end well. Quantifying principles sounds like a guaranteed disaster. Something would get lost in translation. Math might be the language of the world, but not of the soul. In the real world we need to make value judgements, even if this is more art than engineering. We need a set of principles, but how on Earth do we assemble them? How do we get it right? It's a tough problem, starting from the ground up.

Historically, our strategy for this little riddle has been a markedly pragmatic one. Instead of each person reinventing the wheel and determining their own set of values, most people simply follow the leader, or put their trust in their traditions. Our tribal minds, adapted for cooperation in a small group, are not hardwired for active, independent thinking. Applied to the modern world, this herd mentality explains why so many people follow cultural trends without asking tough questions. As it stands now, the rules of modern secular society are both simple and destructive: get a salary, get a mortgage, and, above all, get really comfortable. I mean, live a little, would ya? Sure, that steak was the price of four days' groceries, but you deserve it, and you're having a great time! The dessert menu looks to die for, and another glass of wine would pair nicely with that luscious slice of indulgence on page two. Also, don't ruffle too many feathers—don't make a scene like that guy at the Mexican place yesterday. Just say what you have to in order to get along. In truth, it's a Faustian deal: You are free to have all the cake and unearned virtue you want, but only if you comply with Big Daddy Government.

We've put our tribal trust in corporate leaders and governments to guide society as a group. Like a boat whose parts have been combined for faster locomotion, we too are working together as specialized cogs in a great beast of a machine, creating the kind of raw economic efficiency and perilous speed of consumption that would be laughably unattainable independently. Without the lubrication of high trust and civility in our society, our colossally long, absurdly complicated supply chains would quickly snap under their own weight and our engine would seize. Instead, people keep their heads down, toiling away at some highly specific modern nonsense job, unburdened by the honorable weight of tangible skills, responsibility, or independence. Blindly, we trust that the captain of this ship has a clear destination in mind, and is steering us toward the supposed safety of devoted secularism, obedient globalism, and chronic indulgence.

But do these mainstream leaders really have our best interests in mind? Hard to say, but if the outcome is any indication of intent, then the correct answer is an unambiguous, resounding no. Our vessel, moving at unprecedented speeds, is headed straight for the crag of total dismantlement. Mainstream culture is about to crash in a big way. In the interest of self-preservation, how do we diverge from our current ruinous path? How do we redirect the inertia of our collective consciousness? This inherently slow and energy-intensive process is an immense undertaking. It could take whole generations to convince the deckhands to make a serious course change. The captain definitely isn't changing his mind. Additionally, such an adjustment of vector carries inherent risk: turn too fast and we might tip and capsize, turn too slow, and we fail to avoid smashing into what's ahead. Take a step back and you'll realize that the risk of both extremes is the same: a violent and bloody course correction, where everybody loses.

So, what do we do? Where do we go? How do we manage a non-catastrophic turn of direction? First, we start with the basics. We need to have honorable values, ones that are simple enough to understand for ourselves. No more blindly following poor leadership. With the titanic scale of modern power and money hierarchies, this strategy no longer works. Honest, hard-working citizens need a better understanding of the ethics by which they govern their lives. Putting blind trust in conventional leaders no longer works; our tribe is too big for our chiefs and corporate leaders to maintain a set of balanced principles. When it comes to enormous hierarchies, it appears that honorable values need not apply. In order for would-be leaders to get to the top of these massively competitive, sociopathic pyramids, their personal principles have become so heavily skewed toward a single value, like money or status, as to create—or simply empower—a monster. In the same way that you can't be a clean coalminer, you also can't be an honest, upfront president. Some might try, but when they do, they lose. And it's not even close. Every. Single. Time.

What does all this have to do with Owen Benjamin? What could a gigantic, endearingly crass, goofy comedian nicknamed "Big Bear" possibly have to do with restructuring cultural values? A lot, as it turns out. As recently as just a few short years ago, Big Bear was completely disengaged from the culture war.[7] He was an outlandish comedian working in the heart of the mainstream beast—Los Angeles—obsessed with "crushing" on stage and getting all the high-fives. His specialty was comedy about relationships. Owen would leverage his acute understanding of the interesting differences between men and women to relieve stress with a big round of belly laughs. However, his career took a sharp turn when the culture war formed a battlefield on his territory. Suddenly, it was no longer okay to joke about the differences between men and women because of the cranky postmodernists and their cultural foothold. Their loopy argument that there is literally no difference between men and women began manifesting itself in politics and business. Their absurd attempt at despotism was succeeding—they tyrannically took over universities and businesses. At the forefront of these infested institutions, social justice crazies have advocated for "ladies and gentlemen" to be unironically replaced with "comrades," wishing to label any dissonants with titles like "sexist," "bigot," and "fired."

Owen made a principled stand against the mainstream culture and got ejected from Hollywood for his troubles. For example, when radio-show host Jesse Thorn publicly

---

[7] The culture war is a term that references the ongoing war of ideas: a competition for the consciousness of people to determine what they trust, believe, and act upon.

paraded his two-year-old boy as a transgender girl for social approval, Owen called him out by name. He vocalized such vile behavior for the flagrant child abuse that it is. Long story short, some *"how dare yous"* were aimed at Owen for his troubles. This wasn't an isolated event. Big Bear has consistently said no to enormous social status, money, and power in exchange for maintaining his set of values. Through his actions, Owen has effectively shown that it's not only possible, but advisable to be an honorable man, even in this culture of chronic indulgence and preposterous pseudo-authoritarianism.

Since being kicked off platforms like Facebook, Twitter, and YouTube, Owen has become one of the most important figures in this ongoing culture war. In some ways, it would be nice to not have to endlessly argue about how to behave and restructure society, but like it or not, this war of ideas isn't going away any time soon. The cognitive infrastructure is in place. Unless something dramatic happens, there's going to be indulgent victim consciousness pervading culture for the rest of your life. So get used to it. For years to come, identifying as anything from a pansexual leprechaun to a polyamorous unicorn will be advocated for by the same people who want to teach children about the wonders of trans-humanism and anal bloodplay. American public schools are way worse than people realize. These demons are disgusting. I can hear the green-haired gender-studies major lamenting already: *"How dare you"*

It's up to responsible citizens to honorably engage in uncomfortable ideas and decide for themselves how they will prioritize their values. What will you stand for, and why? On the front line of this fight, Big Bear is putting his high IQ, conflict-seeking temperament, and stunning rhetoric to use. In addition to his natural talent, Owen is an immensely hard worker. Since his medium is livestreaming, he ends up putting out an ocean of video, averaging several hours every day for the past few years. This is both a blessing and a curse. As entertainment, over two thousand hours of interesting archived video content is a blessing for its blend of size and quality. However, some of the more refined points inevitably risk drowning in the sea of content within which it was originally birthed. Consequently, one of the purposes of this book is to distill out some of Owen's rhetoric and store it on paper for safekeeping.

These quotes, and the ideas driving them, are a valuable resource. Like a giant pile of mined gold, it only makes sense to forge these shiny bits together into something cohesive and put it on display. At the turn of his career, when Owen made his thoughtcrime public by simply not changing, he was no longer welcome in the beast of mainstream Hollywood. What did he do to deserve his digital rejection? He spoke out against the chemical castration of Jesse Thorn's little boy, something known by honorable people as being opposed to nauseating child abuse. After his rejection from what we may as well call

Hell on Earth, Owen began working through ideas about basic principles live on air. Shocked into trying to figure out just what the hell is going on in our culture, Owen started at the beginning, clawing tooth and nail through the formidable process of answering the vexing questions posed at the beginning of this chapter: What values are important? Why? To reveal Big Bear's answers to this fickle riddle, this book is split up into chapters that focus on one value at a time, expanding on the arguments that Owen has made over his thousands of hours of video in an order that makes sense.

As a responsible adult, you're obligated to take on this role as well and think about how to govern your life for yourself as well as for your family and community. Ask bigger questions. Empower your mind with the tools of discernment. Whom do you trust? Be responsible. Have principles. What hill would you be willing to die on? Think it through. Decide ahead of time. What lines do you refuse to cross, no matter the consequences? No one can draw these lines for you—*you* have to do it. You have to decide what's important. You have to decide when to take on risk. You have to decide when to reject what's offered. But to do so requires a strong set of values.

> [Money] is like steroids for your soul. It amplifies what you already are, and if you don't have the foundation to handle it,

or if you don't actually have the purpose ready, it just destroys you.

Episode #294

When you're rich, you wake up with the same nightmares; you're just on sheets with a higher thread count.

Some people don't know how bad it can get. If you go down the wrong paths in life, you see the Devil's face.

Episode #831, 1:48:28

It's a blessing and a curse simultaneously, just like everything.

Episode # 776

Don't take the ticket.

I'm not going to give up something of true value for something of no value.

Once bullets start flying, unfortunately everyone's already lost.

There's a price to honesty.

Episode #681

This is what comedy does, guys. I know it seems abrasive to some people . . . but you have to be able to say what people are thinking and can't say. That's our job. That's why I'm getting so trashed . . . I've never been an outsider in society, I've never been an outcast . . . I was always good at my job.

Episode #709

The real N-word is "no."

The animal cannot elevate to the human . . . but the human can degrade to below the animal. Below the animal!

Episode #832, 42:52

That's the problem with not working out your own morality. It leaves you vulnerable. Don't do it for anyone else. Do it for yourself . . . If you let your ideas atrophy, and let your beliefs atrophy, you're manipulatable by anybody with a lot of Twitter followers, or anyone that's giving you an A or an F.

Episode #302

I used to be just a comedian and then when I took the stand against the trans thing in Hollywood, I became a hero and a villain simultaneously. And I took it seriously. That really woke me up to some of the responsibilities in life. I used to just be a comic.

Episode #704

The cavalry isn't coming. It's up to you.

Episode #676

CHAPTER 2

Value of Honesty

Believe it or not, distilling Owen Benjamin's baffling life of extremes into a simple catchphrase wasn't difficult at all. He made the exercise easy when he wrote the thing down in several of his now defunct social media bios. Like a seed, just eight simple words managed to flourish into an entire ethical code, thriving for its honest appeal to nature. Everything from his willingness to endure severe pain and loss to his sobering pursuit of a healthy family to his stalwart commitment to faith in God—all of it is a fractal consequence of one simple, original, forthright ideal: "I might be wrong, but I'm not lying."

This rhetorical phrase is made fascinating by its density. Let's unpack it. What's the only difference between intentionally lying and being unintentionally wrong? It's built right into the adjective: intent. What's so significant about that? If you spend some time and buy some thought, you'll find that the significance of valuing intent is what it implies about *free will*. Intent only matters if free will is genuine. Intentions, goals, and conscious pursuits could only matter in any kind of real or legitimate sense if you have the ability to freely discern between them and make a willful choice. Consider the alternative: an existence of nothing more than being an animated mashup of carbon bits, whose "choices" are nothing more than a predetermined illusory feeling. In such a depressing existence, intent doesn't matter and the game is over. Why should a committed determinist care about the difference between lying and an honest blunder if their life is about as special as a wilting house plant's? Drinking margaritas and playing catch on a beach get old fast. Animalistic pleasures make a poor foundation for building a fulfilling life.

Follow the string of authentic free will and you'll be led to another question: Where does free will come from? So far, the best argument put forth in public discourse that I've seen is the simplest one: As the children of God, living men and women have been given authentic free will through the gift of a divine spark. That's a mic drop. "I might be wrong, but I'm not lying" isn't just a flippant phrase about a preference for honesty, it speaks to a much deeper and more profound core belief system that might as well say, "I am a child of God and I will behave accordingly: passionately pursuing the truth while humbly accepting my own earthly limitations." Owen is a man of rhetoric, however, and such meticulousness doesn't roll off the tongue so well.

Although getting things wrong and lying share the same trait of incorrectness, it would be a mistake to then conflate them as equivalent. Like a blue sky and a blue motorhome, the totality of something is more than just one of its attributes. One is a glorious canvas of aqua blue. The other is a gaudy mistake that should be killed with fire . . . or maybe just repainted. The honesty paradigm is similarly contrasted. While the grace of human limitation includes flaws as an inevitable gift, deliberately lying is just a narcissistic rejection of a principled, moral life. So, here are some questions to now ask yourself: Do you think intent matters? Do you think it's real? Do you think it's genuine? Common law, basic compassion, and honorable principles couldn't function without that inherently subconscious assumption, so it's at least pragmatically correct, but do you—as an individual man or woman—truly believe it? Deep down, what fingerprint do you have personally stamped on the nucleus of your soul? Do you think that there's a difference between a deliberate lie and an honest blunder? Do you see the contrast in this turbulent ether? Do you feel it? The stark distinction between the basic structure of honesty and the basic structure of dishonesty is made inescapable for the immaterial transcendent geometry that shapes it: intent, free will, and the divine spark of God.

One of Owen's paradigm-shifting insights is presented in one of his early videos, "How to understand crazy people." In this old gem, Owen explains why there's been such a rampant emergence of baffling logical contradictions and cognitive dissonance in modern progressive culture. When I first saw this video, the idea was so profound to me that I couldn't believe I hadn't already known about it. The whole thing seemed so obvious and all-encompassing in hindsight that it felt like something I had always been looking at but hadn't stepped back far enough to put its scale in perspective. At the time of this writing, this video can still be found at bitchute.com/video/v2t8-z_TGkg/. However, with Owen's history of having his accounts constantly deleted for his thoughtcrime and the fickle nature of the internet, I feel compelled to write a transcript here.

> "How to understand crazy people," by
> Owen Benjamin

Crazy is a label I once put on women who I broke up with. "She's crazy, I gotta get another girl." And then—what are the odds that this next girl is also crazy? And then, wow! Another crazy one? Well, the definition of crazy is actually doing the same thing over and over again, expecting a different outcome, which is what I was doing. So I took a deep breath, and I tried to start understanding women better. I did! Watch two of my highest-viewed videos, "How to be married and not be murdered," as well as "Gender war." They aren't crazy, they just have different motivations. And I'm now in a very happy marriage and it probably wouldn't have happened if I just kept using the crazy crutch.

So, my next group of people that I assigned the title of *crazy* were the social justice warriors: anyone who agrees with political correctness and, of course, socialists. As time has passed, they haven't gone anywhere, which means either millions of people are just crazy and oddly good at paying their bills, or they have a different motivation that I wasn't seeing. Turns out, just like with women, it was the latter. And I'm finally ready to report. I'm making this video to help the person out there who says, "I'm so confused. Bernie Sanders says guns, prisons, and greed are the problem, and then his solution is that he wants more of our income, or he will send a man with a gun to our house to put us in a jail—these people are crazy!"

Nope, he's not crazy. Neither are the people that say "Caitlyn Jenner is Woman of the Year even though she hasn't been a woman for a full year yet." Or of course, my favorite, "Trump is literally Hitler, now literally give him all your guns because a seventeen-year-old in Florida who looks like the guy from American Pickers said so." So what's their motivation? What makes someone truly say something so paradoxical like, "Only white people can be racist," or, "Gender doesn't exist but it does and there's a wage gap that doesn't exist, but it does." They aren't motivated by the same thing as you or me. You assume everyone wants to figure out the right answer. This was a given in your equation, and it was a mistake. When someone says, "What is two plus two?" we all say, "Four!" But then, it's revealed that if you say five, you will get a piece of candy. I would respond, "But it's four," and they'd say, "But candy," and I'd say, "But it's four." Now, there's a type of person that likes candy more than being right at math. Someone says, "What is two plus two?" and they'd say, "Candy!" I'd say, "But it's four!" and they'd say, "But it's candy."

See, they're both rational, it just depends on what you value. We don't value the same thing. Candy can be social approval, false moral superiority, financial incentives, likes on Facebook, keeping your job, etc. There are millions of people who think it's crazy that anyone would say four. You can't touch truth; you can't eat truth; truth isn't sweet; it sure isn't candy. What kind of person would give up candy for nothing? It's candy. But if you take the candy over what you know to be true, the penalty for accepted lies will only get worse. Being called names that no one expects to be justified with any evidence hurts. "I'm not a homophobe, my dog is gay," you will plead and they will say, "So you now think dogs are gay," and then you *break*. "It's five, okay, it's five, just tell me I'm good. Tell me I love my gay dog."

For most of the world the penalty isn't a thumbs down on YouTube, it's imprisonment or death for not saying five, so it's extra silly to break under such little pressure. The good news is your friendships, your relationships, your business associates will improve dramatically if you hold your ground and you say four. When people know you are the type of person who takes truth over candy, they will allow you much more leeway to make mistakes and evolve your ideas. Your friendships will be much stronger; your business partners will trust you more, which will lead to more and more opportunities, which will lead to more candy. All because they know that when the candyman comes knocking, you'll tell them that you're busy—going to the dentist. That's why the candy people all have to have the exact same opinion on every single issue. Have you noticed that? Everything has to line up or they're out. Because they don't trust each other. That's why the candy people all have the exact same opinion. Because they know that anyone with a bigger Snickers bar or a couple more candy corn will get your loyalty, and your history with that person means nothing if there's more candy corn.

When I think a friend is wrong—I mean horribly wrong, embarrassingly wrong, wrong so my blood boils—I want to argue his point. But my respect for him as a person does not waver. I expect they do the same for me. If I end up realizing that he was right all along, once all my angles and all my arguments have been extinguished, I thank him. Close call; I could have kept being wrong; thanks, good buddy. When I know he knows what's right, and says what will get him candy, that's a sad day for me. Because then I realize the next time we play craps, he may have loaded dice, so I can't trust a victory or learn from a loss, but he really likes candy.

So, I hope that helps you navigate the current chaos. This is much deeper than politics; this is a fundamental issue of a person's motivations and goals. There are a vast amount of people who would rather take candy, even if their agreed-upon lie will give them a toothache in the very near future. They would just say: "But the future isn't now—homophobe." So when they say something like, "Submit to tolerance," and you know they are smart enough to understand that what they just said is a *hilarious* oxymoron, just know they don't care at all. Words are just a means to candy. In their mind, they just said whatever will get to them candy. And once you realize that, you don't take as much offense to what they're saying; you don't take it personally. You don't think that the world is going mad, because it isn't. It's following its rational progress based on human motivation. Some people say four; some people say candy. And once you know that, hopefully you get less stressed. I know I did. Much love, be good, and don't eat too much candy.

Before seeing this video, I was one of the confused people who Owen describes. I subconsciously assumed that everyone was trying—at least on some level—to avoid hypocrisy and seek both logical consistency and the truth. With a new perspective, granted by the gift of knowledge and hindsight, I've experienced a complete paradigm shift. Some people are candy people, plain and simple. They don't care about what's true at all. With a herd mentality, they'll say and do anything for shallow rewards, kicks of dopamine that come in the form of "candy." They completely reject hiking the proverbial hill in pursuit of the value of honesty. Instead, they are preoccupied with the stationary hell of a hedonic treadmill. Like a donkey chasing a carrot on a string, these people will endlessly, maddeningly chase whatever tasty goodies are dangled in front of them, slaves to their own animalistic impulses.

Here's the thing about pursuing truth for the sake of the divine spark: it's an incredibly powerful idea . . . that many will ignore or reject. Some of the more stubborn and secularly minded folks out there need incentives that feel more tangible before they'll be motivated to act. With a history of stubbornness and atheism myself (which was a disaster that we'll cover later), I can personally relate to such cloudy conditions. Luckily for the secular folk, following the laws of God and telling the truth also happens to be the most pragmatic thing to do . . . almost like it's not a coincidence.

What better place to start than trust? As one of the most valuable currencies in the world, building trust should be a priority for anyone. The only effective way to build trust long-term is to be honest. By earning the trust of others, you build better relationships with your friends, business partners, and, most importantly, your family. Everything in life gets better with trust.

Developing trust is about more than just the relationships you have with other people. It's also about the relationship you have with yourself. Even the most convincing liars can't escape their own internal judgement. Liars know they're liars, and no one trusts a liar. Therefore, when it comes to developing trust in yourself, you can't fake it. A liar can't trick themselves into thinking they're trustworthy. It just can't be done. Over time, this erosion of self-trust degrades that person's instincts. They lose their edge. In the sloppy bog of mucky uncertainty, everything slows down. Think of all the benefits you lose out on by impairing your own instincts. Athletes need to trust their instincts when they move, musicians need to trust their instincts when they play, and parents need to trust their instincts with their kids. Any human being dealing with a situation of uncertainty will be much better off with good instincts. Even the tone of your voice will change if you can't trust yourself while speaking, and a disingenuous timbre is something everyone can hear intuitively. With all the deceptive media in the current public square, a huge market has opened up for genuine voices. Owen's skyrocketing success, despite all of the deplatforming, is a testament to this idea that people are ravenous for authenticity, something only honesty and good instincts can provide. Even a selfish secular man or woman can recognize the value of honesty, because everything from your bones to your brain is affected by your instincts— good ones will save your life, bad ones will break you.

One of the things that prevents men and women from beings honest is their shame. There're plenty of people who aren't willing to admit what they've done in the past. This is a two-way street. Really think about this, because it's important: If you know ahead of time that you're committed to being honest, then you stop acting in ways that would later obligate you to lie. It's much easier to be honest about your actions if they aren't shameful acts. If you're not consistently honest, it's time for a reality check: Are your actions moral? What self-improvements would you have to make before you could start speaking honestly about everything you do? Would you feel comfortable publishing your search history for the month?[8] How about for the year? Now you have something to aim for: Act in a way you can be completely honest about.

For every hard truth, there's an easy lie that makes your character just a little bit softer. You can lie to yourself about all kinds of things: why you're constantly angry, why you're always staying late at work, why you're anxious, why you're depressed, why you're fat, why you smoke, why your house is a mess, why your kids don't respect you, why you drink, why your marriage is vacant, why you get angry,

---

[8]   It's worth noting that this isn't an argument for puritanical openness by the way. You can have privacy without being dishonest. "That's none of your business, my friend," is a perfectly acceptable, perfectly honest answer to many questions. However, the point stands: if your search history is shameful, you're doing something wrong.

why you watch "the pornos," why you have consumer debt, or why you have a habit of wasting so much time brainlessly staring into a screen. In dishonorable situations like these, it's easier to lie about your failures than it is to be honest about why you fail. Taking the easier path, people who lie to themselves about their gluttony, lust, pride, sloth, wrath, envy, or greed have abandoned the deterrent of what follows from honesty. Liars deflect for the weakness of their character; a head-on collision with the truth requires strength. Instead of facing hard truths directly, dishonest men and women aim their rage out and blame others. "How dare you fat shame?" says fat Tina. "I'm a victim. I need these cakes. I need these bagels. You're a bigot." Rather than stoically addressing their own faults, the morally mushy indignantly claim that it's society that needs to accept every form of character flaw, no matter how repulsive or lazy. Fortunately for those who aspire to something better, there's an alternative: honest self-reflection, developing the moral strength necessary to honorably face the hard truths of personal shortcomings, and then actually doing something about it.

These four basic tenets—trust, instincts, morality, and strength—can serve to reframe the way we think about the value of honesty. Specifically, about how a principled commitment to honesty develops over time. The most valuable benefits of honesty don't just happen overnight. Building trust, sharpening instincts, thriving morally, and bulking your strength of character are all lifelong processes. Development is a feedback loop. It builds on itself, feeding its own algorithm as it grows, and grows, and grows. It can take years before the commitment to honesty starts paying back substantial dividends. Instead of thinking about honesty like the illumination of a lightbulb, think of it like a years-long sunrise. Flicking a switch might provide an immediate kickback, but an LED makes a poor replacement for the glory of a solar zenith. The revolution of the value of honesty comes in degrees. Bit by bit, anyone can drag themselves out of the dark, but they have to commit to trusting in the process of slowly building the light.

Although the serious benefits of honesty require patience to fully express themselves, time isn't the only important factor. What's also critical is to understand that there isn't an option to go in halfway. "I might be wrong, but I'm not lying" is distinct from "I might be wrong, but I'm *usually* not lying." The algorithm of honesty is only effective if you believe ahead of time that you will hold yourself accountable to your own actions. The feedback part of the feedback loop requires willful authenticity. You have to plant your feet and honorably face hard truths head on. Otherwise, self-deception forms a habit that tends to spiral out of control. If you leave yourself the backdoor trap of lying for candy, then you might find you forget all about the front door.

Before we move on, I want to quickly address a point of criticism that some of the more scrupulous readers may now have. In chapter 1, I put forward an argument: Being a complete person requires embracing multiple values. However, here in chapter 2, I've now argued that it's best to fully commit to the value of honesty and truth, which could seem like a pretty glaring contradiction that's worth clarifying. Think about it this way: You're building a house of values. As a construction project, one of your most important goals is to build an exceptionally solid, plumb foundation. Honesty, and the pursuit of truth is your foundation. "I might be wrong, but I'm not lying" is your base. Build on that. The critical idea to understand here is that a superb foundation doesn't take anything away from the rest of the building *as long as you pursue it in the context of a construction project.* If you break out a precision laser level and a rainbow of sandpaper grits then spend the rest of your life building the flattest foundation this world has ever seen, you'll die with nothing to show for it but a smooth chunk of rock in the ground. If your purpose is building a house, then build a house.[9]

Whether conscious or not, even an earnest commitment to the value of honesty will include saying

---

[9]   If spending forever finding perfect proverbial level sounds like your thing, power to ya. You should know, though, that there's a decent chance you'll end up alone in the woods somewhere fighting the government over obscure laws that no one cares about. Or you might become a legend who's really fond of pigeons and invents everything for the next few generations. That could happen too—you never know.

things that are a shade off from what you most honestly believe. Conversations with a best friend look a lot different than those with a stranger. That's just reality. People say things to get along. However, civility isn't an excuse to abandon ardent honesty. I have some rules that I like to uphold to manage this conundrum: I make every effort to be as direct and transparent as the circumstance allows, I never, ever speak what I believe to be false, and I don't cast pearls before swine. "*How dare you*" says the swine. Using civility as a replacement for the value of honesty is just a feeble, self-soothing obfuscation that people use to resign from the challenge of honorably speaking what they believe to be true.

In closing, trying to cover all the benefits of committing to honesty and the pursuit of the truth would be like trying to cover all the benefits of committing to a sturdy foundation that prevents collapse. As a construction manager, that would be the easiest pitch meeting ever: "What do you want? A safe house or a dead family? Good aesthetic or rubble? A cost-effective home or an expensive disaster? Think about it then get back to me before we get started on your house." Such a list can go on just as long as your imagination will allow it to, because the subject matter is so fundamental. Nobody considers intentionally building a bad foundation, that's crazy. It would be like wondering whether or not it's a good idea to have a beating heart or a working brain.

Part of what makes a discussion about honesty such a challenge is that we're tribal thinkers. We like our beliefs to be in a box, where the thought is presented as a strict binary, gift-wrapped with a pretty bow. Many people aren't receptive to the finicky nature of nuance. They don't care about the intricacies of an idea. They just want to know which tribe the speaker is coming from so that they can either reject the position of that speaker out of hand with some righteous indignation, (*how dare you*) or be an ardent blind supporter of such infinite wisdom. [10] For this reason, convincing someone to change their mind face to face can be a challenge. Breaking away from a tribal idea is easier to do if that listener is actively consenting to listen, and it's not always obvious which concepts a listener is receptive to exploring. Without that basic framework, pushing harder doesn't work. If someone isn't open to an idea in person, beating them over the head with it isn't helpful. Unfortunately, when hard, stern words fall on soft, deaf ears, it's usually a lose-lose. Even if it's true. Not everyone can compartmentalize well, and unloading your worldview on someone without consent isn't, shall we say, kosher. A book solves this problem nicely. I can write all my most controversial ideas down, and if you don't like

---

[10] This is why people say things like, "I don't agree with everything Owen says." It vocalizes their ultimate allegiance to the mainstream tribe, giving them something to fall back to, fleeing from the "how dare yous."

them, go ahead and close the book. Or burn it. I don't care. The point is, by writing it down, nobody gets to learn these ideas without actively consenting to explore them.

Let's suppose now that someone is open to pursuing the truth. They're committed to seeking a strong moral character and fully embracing the value of honesty as best they can to live a complete life. That's fantastic. Embracing honesty is just the first step towards speaking the truth however, because determining what is actually true is a whole challenge unto itself. Learning how to understand the truth of things in an appropriate context is a skill that requires practice and competence to be effective. We've got a word for this process: *discernment.*

> Everyone sins. But sin just means miss the mark. And the whole reason that's important is you have to believe there's a mark.

> What is true is God, there is no difference.

> Someone speaking what they believe to be true [has] a really nice vibration. It feels good. It's healing.

> If your purpose is fun, your life is just slowly ending. The party is slowly just

going to dwindle away and you will enter oblivion once the music stops playing.

Episode #169

That's the problem with living in the illusion world. A lot of those people don't even know why they're crying every day. When you start taking those tickets of lies, you can't even do a self-diagnosis anymore.

Episode #831, 22:30

It's an honor to have someone's trust.

Episode #536

If you don't trust your voice, you'll lose your instincts.

You can't make a deal with morality.

When you live lies, you can't confront any truth.

Episode #536

Be unapologetically strong.

Have an iron will.

The thing that saved me in life was to stop lying.

Episode #231

You have to stand up for exactly what you believe in at all times and never waver.

Think about how many people that are thinking about shooting themselves in the brain and then, when told enough truth, they don't—that's literally curing someone of a terminal illness called depression and despair.

Episode #778 (bonus)

Evil is: I might be lying but I'm not wrong.

More honesty quotes:

You have to look at the world as it really is.

Episode #215

35

When people live a lie, they only have two options: either admit you're a liar or start believing your own lie.

Episode #242

People are sick of being lied to. And even if you don't admit the big lies, that's fine. Just don't call me names, and don't try to evangelize on my channel. That's all I ask.

If you're building your identity on sand, you're capable of anything [terrible].

It's okay to be wrong. It's not okay to be knowingly wrong.

It is not brave to speak the Truth. It's like saying it's brave to drink water. No. If you don't drink water, you die.

If you don't condemn it, you're part of it. I'm not here to stop it; I can't stop it. I don't have the ability. But what I do have is the ability to speak the truth.

What's brutal about honesty? Why don't people say, "You're brutally lying"?

There's nothing brutal about my honesty. My honesty is kind . . . When I say things, it's not because I'm trying to hurt you . . . honesty will save your life.

Episode #687

Let go of what you want and embrace what is.

The first moment you agree to nonsense, people own you.

Episode #160

Don't be a messenger for the wrong message.

Episode #559

Every moment of every day, you can get off the train . . . it's never over . . . as you're dying, with your last breath, you can say something true.

Episode #555

My angle is truth.

Episode #558

Everyone is brilliant if you just stop lying.

Episode #547

Honesty makes you less vulnerable.

Episode #540

A liar has no value.

Truth exists outside of yourself.

There's no irony in a world with no truth.

I highly recommend people live honest lives.

We see truth through a cloudy glass.

Truth over tribe.

You have no value to the world if you aren't willing to say stuff that gets you hated.

Some people don't speak the language of truth.

Your ignorance isn't helping anybody.

I need people that can see.

You have a right to be wrong.

None of us are truly awake.

I'm open-minded until I'm not.

If you can't argue the other side, you don't know enough to talk.

You're only as sick as your secrets.

The difference is people who pursue truth and people who pursue power.

If the truth shames you, and you kneel, you freeze in your existence."

Episode #721

Don't watch the news. You'll get more truth from C.S. Lewis.

If you live in lies, they always come back . . . If I didn't have less fear in me now, and

39

if I wasn't more peaceful and in a more logos-driven life, I wouldn't have known that even existed. So many people are living their life always short of breath. Their heart rate is always ten beats too fast and then don't even know it. They're just reacting.

Episode #714

We need to start telling truth in this age of lies.

Episode #292

Don't pretend to be something you're not, because eventually you'll start to believe the lie.

Episode #290

If you let someone control your words, your logos . . . they can control your mind.

Episode #660

Not [naming] the Devil is how he controls you.

Episode #273

Such a haunting lullaby. It's so haunting. That's why I like honesty. Was it made by someone who was a bad guy? Yeah. But even when you're honest about being a bad guy, there's value in it.

Episode #694

I'm motivated by truth, because if you don't have a grasp on the truth, you are not funny.

Episode #726

When you hear something true, you feel less alone.

Episode #723

I'm not a power guy; I'm a truth guy. When someone this corrupt and disgusting says something true, I will highlight it and show it to people. Because I don't care about power; I care about the truth."

Episode #763

There's a price to be paid when you speak the truth.

Episode #663

I just say what I see.

Episode #655

CHAPTER 3

Value of Discernment

If you've never heard the blind men and the elephant parable, then you're in for a treat. The story goes like this: A few blind men are introduced to an elephant for the first time. They've never seen one before and have no idea what to expect. Each of the sightless men touches part of the elephant, sculpting a statue that fills the canvas of his mind. One man touches the elephant's trunk: his mind hatches a rugged snake. One man touches the elephant's tail: his mind sews a sinewy rope. One man touches the elephant's leg: his mind grows a leathery tree. For their unique experiences, they each walk away with unique perspectives. Next, the men all sit down to discuss. They try to answer the vexing question: What is an elephant?

For a sighted man, with the advantage of seeing the bigger picture, the question seems trivial, absurd even. Isn't it obvious that an elephant is all these parts combined? Not at all. Perspectives are shaped by their original assumptions. The blind men don't imagine such a colossal creature because the limitation of their senses wasn't able to present one. For the purpose of the parable, all these men knew was the small section of elephant that they were able to scrutinize. In their minds, the portion of the elephant that they touched was the whole elephant. Each man, subordinate to a smaller scale, mistakes his piece of the puzzle for the whole thing.

In some versions of the story, the blind men overcome their limitations and varied viewpoints. As honest, moral men with high trust in each other, they were able to expand their frame of reference to accommodate their conflicting perspectives. Such success required a stalwart commitment to the value of honesty; trust was a necessary precondition to overcome uncertainty. In this winning version of the parable, the blind men were able to exercise humility and cooperate with each other to see the bigger picture. Accomplishing this commendable success isn't easy, however. Since many people aren't honest, working together to form a bigger picture is a nonstarter. No one knows who is lying to whom, and all you have is a giant mess. Dishonesty rots the seed before it has a chance at growth. Even perfect logic is ineffective if built on a foundation of erroneous assumptions, like overlooking the pull of "candy." However, lying isn't the only path to falsehoods; honest people get things wrong all the time too. Sometimes the problem is the facts. Other times the problem is the frame.

In unsuccessful versions of the story, the blind men, although honest, default to the path of least resistance. They fail to acknowledge their own limitations, choosing stubbornness over humility. Instead of bringing their perspectives together in a harmonized chorus, they clash in raucous dissonance. These men foolishly argue amongst themselves over whose single view is the entire truth. Is an elephant like a snake, a rope, or a tree? These incompetent versions of the blind men fail to discern the appropriate resolutions for their individually correct facts. By fighting for the same place on the board, their cognitive puzzle pieces are competing vertically instead of connecting horizontally. In some versions of the story the men even kill each other over this misoriented feud. Although this parable has several versions, the fundamental message of each is the same: Discerning the truth requires honesty, correct facts, *and* appropriate perspectives.

As individual human beings, we simply can't understand everything in its totality. That is a fundamental, inescapable truth about the human condition: it's undeniable that we are limited. The world is too big and too complex for any one of us to understand it entirely. Just like the blind men and the elephant, we must put our little facts in a large frame; we must trust and cooperate with each other if we wish to understand the bigger picture. But trust must be earned, and cooperation is for those with similar goals. If the goal of discovering truth is the agreed upon destination, then the first step is to make a conscious decision to be honest. What logically follows is the need for discernment so that honest facts can be put in their appropriate frames, combining into the truth. But make no mistake, navigating the path of discernment is a real challenge. It never really ends either. Big Bear, who specializes in understanding complex patterns and explaining them with simple, hilarious rhetoric, has spent thousands of hours on camera actively working through ideas. And he's not stopping anytime soon. There's always more to the tapestry of reality for you to learn about if you're willing to put in the work. Such intelligent discernment, however, is the exception rather than the rule. Pop in a college discussion group (I guess that would be online now), and you'll find that arguments have become breathtakingly stupid, because school has become void of discernment.

Refusing to allow arguments to speak for themselves has become the status quo. The modern conversation is the loser version of the blind-men parable. Do you believe the elephant is like a snake or like a tree? What side are you on? What party line do you toe? What camp are you in? Put yourself in a box: ally or adversary. A hundred or zero. Black or white. It's this kind of bimodal thinking that has contributed to creating such a disaster of depressed consciousness. Forget understanding different perspectives or making any serious attempt to cooperate in a diligent pursuit of the greater, overall truth. Instead, be dishonest for the greater cause of the tribe. Get angry, pop off a few "how dare yous," and commit to the stupidity of false binaries and category errors.[11] One of us is dead wrong, and it's you. Obviously an elephant is like a snake and not like a tree. Bigot. That's the state of what's trendy right now: arrogant, indignant, brain-dead false righteousness. We can do better.

Disentangling this unmitigated trainwreck of failures won't be easy, however. For our culture's commitment to fervent crayon binging and pooping rainbows, nuanced discernment is a big ask. Because discernment deals in context, overcoming the stupidity of extremes doesn't mean embracing centrism. Let me explain. The average

---

[11]   A "false binary" is a decision which misleadingly presents two options as the only options. "Would you like to read *How Dare You* quickly or slowly?" assumes reading my book, which no one is obligated to do (thanks for reading, by the way). A "category error" is classifying something with the wrong category, e.g., an elephant leg fits the category of "elephant part," not "elephant".

between two extremes isn't the correct answer by default. Accommodation isn't a virtue for its own sake. You can consider contrasting perspectives and their different applications without compromising between the two. Discernment isn't about splitting the difference, it's about thinking in a more refined way to get closer to the totality of the truth. You don't have to double your IQ to discern, either. You just have to learn to see how context influences the appropriateness of application. Different perspectives are like different tools: everyone has a toolkit they can use, and you don't need the perfect toolkit to build something great. All it takes is a bit of practice. Even just a hammer and a string are enough to do wonders if you learn how they work. Seeing the value in both tools means learning how to use them separately. Trying to compromise between the two by fabricating a hammer out of string creates naught but a useless monstrosity. That's centrism.

If you want your ideas to be more than a perpetually limping compromise, you're required to elevate your consciousness and see the world more judiciously. Discernment about life is like solving a puzzle with more pieces than there are spots on the board. Some pieces go on the board and some go in the trash. This mismatch of pieces and places introduces a tricky element to the game. When a piece doesn't fit, is the appropriate response rejection or reorientation? If a few more blind men show up and start picking up bricks and turtles, how can they know to reject those perspectives as part of the elephant? Some ideas are worth incorporating. Other ideas are just hot garbage and should be incinerated as such.[12] Discerning between the two is the challenge. Open your mind too much and your brain will fall out. Close your mind too much and your brain will suffocate. Compromise too much and your toolkit doesn't work. What a mess.

To further complicate things, we'll need to address the issue of binaries, continuums, and proximity to the truth. It's important to know that this entire worldview that I'm presenting assumes the existence of one greater, overall truth, where the human interpretation of that great truth is limited. With this perspective, the pursuit of truth is an asymptotic one: one long, enlightening journey of context, nuance, and convergence on something technically unattainable. Let's try putting some of these ideas together in a discerning thought experiment about something simple: what's black and what's white. It doesn't get any more obvious than the difference between black and white. However, *sigh,* not everyone agrees. "Draw a precise line between black and white on a spectrum," sneers the academic postmodernist. "You can't do it because the category of black and white is just a construct in your mind." Tiresomely, this is true. The category of black and the category of white just helps us communicate with each other. Light exists within a spectrum, not a series of discrete categories, except in our own minds.

---

[12]   Don't burn the turtles!

We invent discrete colors like black and white because the continuum of black to gray to white isn't something our minds categorize intuitively. Even just describing it required me to break it up into buckets: black, gray, and white. But where are the precise lines that define the exact separation? What is gray? What about halfway between black and gray? Is that blackish-gray? You could split that hair forever. To communicate, we simplify things. Describing different parts of a light spectrum requires consciously separating it into chunks, which doesn't represent how it fundamentally functions in nature. We blur out the complexity to manufacture the simplification. We step away from the details so we can understand the abstraction.

The deconstructionist postmodernist then uses this argument to assert that since moral concepts are mental constructs, they're not real, and can be rejected. They say that honesty and dishonesty are puzzle pieces we can chuck out: "Do what you want; it's all made up anyway." This is a mistake of resolution. If you force the right fact into the wrong frame, the ultimate picture doesn't make sense. Nobody can give a good answer to the question, "Which square foot of this creature is an elephant?" because the frame of reference makes it impossible. A trunk is not an elephant. Neither is a tail. It doesn't mean elephants don't exist. The problem is just a framing issue. Moral values are the same. They exist in a continuum that we describe using distinct terms because that's the way our minds work. "Black" and "white" are a poor way of framing the light spectrum in a fundamental sense, but that doesn't mean the underlying phenomenon doesn't exist. We're just limited in the way we categorize it. We break things down into "moral" and "immoral" or "honest" and "dishonest" because the oversimplification is simple enough to understand. We prefer to think of these things as binaries even though the transition between the two is a gradation. In this way, sometimes what we think of as a precise binary is really just a pragmatic description of the two extreme ends of a continuum. Choosing pragmatism over precision doesn't dismantle the concept or make it any less real, it just readjusts the frame of resolution to something that doesn't perfectly fit the phenomenon. And there's nothing wrong with that.

It's not difficult, or enlightening, to be a deconstructionist postmodernist. All they do is dump an unreasonable burden of proof onto good people. They ask for a perfect description of the nuanced totality of morality, then claim victory when such an overwhelming demand is not met. For example, a postmodernist will reject the idea that it is immoral to cheat on your wife on the grounds that it is difficult to precisely define where the line between cheating and not cheating is. Backrub? Cheek kiss? Porn? Is it the emotional intent? Is it the physical act? Are there exceptions? As you can probably guess, there's no shortage of people who find deconstructionist types irksome. I know I do. How deconstructionists frame the argument is a problem. They take this confusion surrounding continuums and use it to scapegoat the morality issue. They claim that if you can't define a precise line between morality and immorality then the whole concept itself is somehow illegitimate. Nonsense. They're chasing their tails.

Esoteric drivel about mental constructs is the tool of an immoral man seeking to justify or validate his immoral behavior. Alternatively, a moral man doesn't attempt to deconstruct morality. He doesn't resort to these kinds of tricky postmodernist philosophies because he's genuinely trying to do the right thing. A moral man simply admits his own limitations and forthrightly aims up as best he can. He can feel what's right and what's wrong even if he can't write a dissertation about it. He knows that both actions and intent matter. He knows that consciously aiming for the light is different than aiming for the dark, regardless of the finicky transition between the two. He knows that when he falls short of his goal, the appropriate response isn't to glorify or excuse his fall, but to shake off the dirt and try even harder. Discernment doesn't mean rejecting simple concepts, it means recognizing them as pragmatic representations of something more complicated. There's no shortage of smart people with bad ideas. And just because something is complex doesn't mean it's correct. In fact, a sign of intelligence is taking something convoluted and explaining it in simple terms.

Like driving, the best resolution is often more practical than it is precise. The "right place" and "wrong place" for two cars on the road aren't separated by inches, they're separated by feet. Being unable to point at the exact inch that separates the constructed binary of the "right place" and the "wrong place" on the road doesn't somehow dismantle the idea that it would be better to not crash the car. Developing discernment means learning to utilize either resolution when appropriate. Learning to zoom in and learning to zoom out. Comfort with complexity and savoring simplicity. Sometimes it's helpful to talk about black and white (don't cheat on your wife by having sex with other women), while other times it's helpful to talk about the whole gradient (don't even come close to cheating on your wife—her emotional security is important, so ditch your precious pornos). One perspective doesn't somehow dismantle the other. These different resolutions are just tools to help us think and, more importantly, act. Discerned facts are connected to their deliberate frames. Sometimes it's best to zoom out, and then zoom out again and again if necessary, to get the whole picture. Other times, it's enlightening to zoom in. Depending on the context, the best advice for life might require thousands of hours of dedicated, deep analysis on honorable values from a brash, intelligent comedian. Other times, "try harder" will do.

Let's do a strange little exercise. Here's a question for a tedious thought experiment about discernment: How tall are you? For myself, if I'm feeling particularly optimistic, I measure six foot nothin' in the morning. But is that my height? Even if I walk around at five eleven after some good ol' axial compression of Mr. Lumbar, can I still claim the height of six feet tall because that is my height at some point in the day? Maybe I can do it on a technicality, but it's a gray area at best. Ninety-nine percent of my day is spent at five eleven. I consider it misleading to claim six feet because it would be a deliberate obfuscation of the intended question: "What height are you *most of the time*?" It's the difference between answering the low-resolution, common-parlance version of the question and trying to be a bit of a sneak and getting away with sounding taller than I am without technically lying. For the honorable human being, it's immoral to mislead on a technicality. The intent of a moral man is to convey the truth for its own sake, not leverage a correct fact for his own ends. As you can see, however, enough precision will introduce tedious complexity. Here's reality: You aren't one height. The simple question deliberately ignores the fact that you take on a range of heights throughout the day as well as throughout your life. If you wanted to get wicked nerdy on this whole thing, you could answer the question by taking a bunch of measurements at regular time intervals, create a distribution, do a little dork analysis, and get ridiculed as a dweeb for eternity after you share it. I'm good. I'll pass. Nobody does this in real life because it's silly. Also, to avoid the social shame. It zooms in *waaay* past the intended resolution of the question to a perspective that is a colossal waste of time. When people talk about height, it's just a hockey bro who wants to tell his buddies about the ogre on the ice the other day, a woman who wants to know if she can wear heels to the blind date on Saturday, or a man the size of a bear who makes people laugh by yelling into a microphone about how short men shaped like overgrown toes kick him in the shin. Nobody cares about getting so precise with a question about stature that the "true" answer requires a height distribution.

It's a bit of a silly example, but it nonetheless re-illustrates an important point. In this pursuit of the value of discernment, there's an interplay between being precise and being pragmatic. With precision, if you get too carried away and super-nerd the resolution, the whole ordeal can spiral out of control. Like this height example, rules for a culture can appear nonsensical when dialed right down to an individual man at an individual moment. It takes a discerning mind to see different forms of context, like the fact that what you do now affects what happens later, that what you do as an individual affects the whole group, and that principles, systems, and algorithms are a completely different resolution than an isolated, individual choice.

Addressing these differences is difficult. Language is limiting. I make all kinds of sweeping claims in this book. I'll say things that make sense for a group of people if they're moral, but don't make sense for a group of people if they're immoral. I'll say things that make sense as a long-term rule that won't make sense for an isolated exception in the moment. I'll say things that apply to a demographic you're a part of but won't make sense for you as an individual. I can't express these resolutions simultaneously because of my limitations as a living man. As an author, it's my job to write with impact and avoid getting lost in the weeds of modifiers: *some* people, *often* honest, speak *part* of the truth. Talk about bland. Instead, taking after the Big Bear, I'll just speak with conviction, and whatever happens next, happens next. Honest men speak the truth. I might be wrong, but I'm not lying. As a man with moral intent, it's my job to ensure that my ideas are written with altruism, honesty, and discernment. As a reader, it's your job to make an earnest attempt to see the arguments I make through the appropriate lens. If I'm speaking about a certain idea and leave out the tiresome tangent about how it doesn't apply to everyone for everything at everytime,[13] it's a mistake on your part to get personally offended. "How dare you" is the mantra of the habitually undiscerning.

To demonstrate my point about the importance of context and discernment, I'll use the most extreme example I can think of. Consider the typical social justice warrior, or SJW. This demographic is the perfect example of what happens when you burn discernment. The whole thing is taking a great value, compassion, and mutating

---

[13]   Let's add "everytime" to the dictionary.

it with the wrong context. SJWs scream about nonsense, reject any hint of logical consistency, and advocate for legislation that is dismantling society in a catastrophic race to the bottom. It's the kind of loony infestation that forces a system reset. However, the purported mission statement of the SJW can be boiled down to a surprisingly reasonable directive: Care about the downtrodden. That's it. Simple, compassionate, and sensible. On its own, at its most abstract level—zoomed *waaay* out—the purported SJW credo is perfectly sane. So what's the problem? How does it spiral so far out of control into such a horrendous abomination? What's interesting is that the answer to this contradiction doesn't reveal a surprising paradox or bizarre anomaly, but a predictable, logical, and inevitable consequence of scale. It's taking something that should only exist in one domain and attempting to expand it to another where it has no business operating. They're swatting flies with bazookas, wondering why the house is falling down. The failure of the application of the SJW credo is a failure to discern that compassion doesn't scale well as an algorithm up to the institutional level. If you want your fellow human beings to smile, punishing frowns with the death penalty is not exactly the best move.

At risk of contradicting my earlier statement about modifiers, *many* SJWs are not motivated by compassion in any sense. For them, alignment with the SJW credo is merely a tactic for malicious, narcissistic, morally bankrupt self-advancement. However, I'll stand by my earlier statement: The basic, most abstract, abused principle that fuels low-ranking SJWs is their compassion. Many of the casual SJWs that I've met genuinely think they're doing super-duper good by babying adults. This is where discernment comes in. Their application of compassion is inappropriate. Acknowledging that compassion itself is an admirable value and that the SJW philosophy is based on compassion, doesn't mean I'm then posturing to align with their tribe. The total is not the sum of its parts. SJWs and I could not be more opposite. I believe in fostering strength; SJWs believe in caring for weakness. I believe in taking on more responsibility; SJWs believe in forcing more rights. I believe in stoicism; SJWs believe in outrage. I believe in rewarding competence and merit; SJWs believe in equity legislation. I believe in the hard lessons of failure; SJWs believe in infantilizing adults. Everything, and I mean *everything* about the SJW philosophy is about as antithetical to my belief system as something could possibly be. In my eyes, they're demons. "*How dare you!*" say the demons. When I argue against the SJW political movement, it isn't because I'm a heartless robot, it's because I understand the appropriate and, more importantly, inappropriate application of compassion. Compassion is about the *inter*personal, not the *im*personal. The focus of my belief system is a perspective that is most appropriate for the context of large groups, entire cultures, and social order as a system. The SJW philosophy of equity, victim consciousness, and uncompromising compassion is only good for dealing with literal babies. The serious SJWs fail to discern appropriate context because they aren't even trying. Their intent isn't to figure out what's true. Lying is a critical part of the SJW ethic.[14] Discernment isn't one of their values at all. Not even close.

For anyone seeking an honorable existence, discernment is a value worth pursuing, however difficult it may be. We don't naturally think in abstract continuums, we think in terms of categories that aren't on a spectrum, like *men* and *women*, because it's more practical.[15] In contrast, a sluggish, nuanced transition of gray is what separates black from white. Luckily, where perfect discernment fails, intent can compensate. Lines in the sand are either arbitrary or obvious, depending on the resolution. When unsure of where to draw, we fall back on our basic values. Without a strong, conscious pursuit of the value of honesty, it can be easy to slide down a slippery slope, incrementally descending to dishonesty. People don't just say exactly what's on their mind all the time. We give each other space to speak. We let things go out of respect when necessary. We intuit what's appropriate for the circumstances. We do things to get along. Everybody has a filter out of social necessity, but filters get clogged.

---

[14] Check out Vox Day's book, *SJWs Always Lie: Taking Down the Thought Police.*

[15] The technical category for men and women is a bimodal distribution.

They're not ideal. Values that disrupt the flow of truth create mucky situations. The less filtered the better.

And so, we move on with the intent of being as transparent and honest as possible through our discernment. Recognizing that what appears to be a contradiction of facts may just be a contradiction of frame is revealing. Remembering that failures of perfect discernment can rely on the crutch of good intent is encouraging. Realizing that we operate in degrees of distance from the truth is enlightening. Of course, sometimes people just get things wrong, and not in that gray-zone kind of way either. In this great big puzzle of the world that we're building, we've got more pieces than we know what to do with, and it's a fact that some are better left out. There's no shortage of bad questions, bad answers, and bad contradictions that are simply wrong. Disasters are everywhere. Look around and you'll find every kind of abysmal idea: Smell-O-Vision, hair in a can, sauna pants. Yep, *sauna pants*. Sometimes, context just isn't the problem. Look at a tortoise any way you want; it'll never be a part of an elephant.[16] The purpose of this chapter isn't to posture for moral relativism, claim that every idea is somehow a good one, or justify speaking with a filter. The purpose is to deliberately pursue a higher degree of

---

[16]   Unless a few geneticists with some screws loose make a bad call and manage to hatch up some kind of turt-a-phant abomination. It could happen.

consciousness and a clearer mind. If you can learn from the blind men and the elephant, then you stand a better chance of seeing the bigger picture. Sometimes one part of the greater truth can appear, falsely, to conflict with another. Without discernment, it's easy to become blinded by what you can already see.

One of the decisions you'll have to make with discernment is the tradeoff between precision and pragmatism. Imperfection isn't an excuse to abandon discernment. You don't need to conduct a statistical analysis of your height to qualify as honest and truthful about your stature, because the resolution of the answer need only match the resolution of the question. Honest intent solves this silly problem, anyhow. We pragmatically operate within the bounds of our own limitations, and that's perfectly okay. Zoom out far enough and the entire dartboard effectively becomes a bullseye. Zoom in far enough, and you're not playing darts anymore. Any attempt to reach the truth will inevitably result in varying degrees of success or failure. Off-white is as good as you'll ever get, which isn't an invitation to give up aiming for the light. With discernment, you get to enjoy your own limitations while attempting to put things in perspective as best you can, learning to appreciate honest views that would otherwise repudiate your own. The contradictions that pop up between logic and compassion, for example, don't mean that one's always right and one's always wrong, it just means that the appropriateness of their application varies with the context. Like a hammer and string, different tools have different uses. Acknowledging the value of both doesn't require centrism, it requires honest discernment. And if you're going to be honest and discerning, you're just going to have to learn to grapple with these confusing issues. You'll have to find the humility, and the humanity, to appreciate honest perspectives that differ from your own while simultaneously reserving the ability to disagree.

This illuminating process of discernment requires seeing more. For many, the exposure to so much light is uncomfortable. That's the hard, honest truth. However, it's much better to embrace the discomfort of wrestling with a challenging idea than to take the easy way out. Why is that? To a real wrestler, "no pain, no gain" sounds like an obvious trope or truism about life. Great athletes love to make it hurt. To most people, however, siphoning blood, sweat, and tears into the earth isn't exactly their idea of a good time. If how most people act is any indication of how they think, then comfort may as well be declared a supreme virtue for the modern era, commandment number one in the sad, undiscerning holy book of contemporary secularism. It almost begs the question: What's the value in voluntarily embracing discomfort?

> We all just have perspectives. We are not
> the mouthpieces of truth.

Episode #757

They're so hyper-specialized that they don't see the forest through the trees.

Episode #708

If you're not honest about the situation, you can't even begin to solve it. There's just no way.

Episode #762 (bonus)

Like the blind men touching the elephant, we all need each other's perspective to figure out what's going on here.

Episode #745

We act out narratives and we don't know where they're from. There is a way out. There is a way to be more discerning. There is a way to enjoy this beautiful and wonderful existence and be grateful . . . but it's challenging.

Episode #710

If you have to attack the person and not the idea, you're weak.

Episode #266

I don't believe in middle ground. I'm not a moderate. I'm not center. I think center doesn't exist. I think you might as well say you're a coward.

Episode #288

Trust your instincts. Go back to what you see and know is true.

Episode #661

They only give you tenure when you're broken.

Episode #263

Know the difference between being convinced of a new thing and being manipulated.

Episode #229

Evil uses black and white a lot. The forced binary.

Episode #747

A lion would love it if there were no [perceived] differences between lions and zebras.

They're still wrestling with a contradiction that's not a contradiction.

Episode #691

If you just let me wander, I'm going to go down some strange paths.

I can't be responsible for the worst interpretation of my words.

Some people aren't like that. [When some people] find out they are wrong, they get defensive, they project, they gaslight, they make other people feel crazy . . . that's cancerous. All you do is limit your ability to feel the outside world.

Episode #303

You can't legislate morality.

I would only debate with someone who is truly trying to find the right answer.

Episode #722

It's not about where your line is, it's do you have one?

Episode #804, 56:45

It's not an IQ situation, it's a problem of discernment. People have been failed. They've been entertained to death.

Episode #663

My tribe is people that when you make a good point, they look excited, not threatened.

Episode #244

In paradise, it's easy to become stupid.

Episode #288

More discernment quotes:

> It's almost impossible for most people to discern lies from truth.

Episode #757

> What is a leader? . . . A leader is someone you follow. Don't follow, and there's no leader.

Episode #714

> If you focus on the trauma of your ancestors, you can't live your life properly.

Episode #716

> I got this knowledge from scars. I wasn't born with this knowledge; it didn't just strike me like lightening. I have scars.
>
> The lower case "i," the insignificant narcissist.

Episode #718

Money doesn't mean shit if there's someone who will just burn your house down. Don't do that.

Episode #656

There is a lot you don't know.

You can always have financial freedom if you just have less shit.

I don't want to give away my children's money. I don't want to sell my kids' future because I want stuff for free.

Start thinking long-term . . . everything isn't automatic. Don't eat the marshmallow immediately. Think long-term. Long-term you have to have children. Stable, community, skills. You're not defined by your stuff. Then you're fine. All their weapons don't work if you do that.

Episode #714

Why would you want to homogenize your information base?

Episode #704

I felt like I was in a madhouse.

Episode #291

This isn't an issue of offensive jokes, it's an issue of right and wrong.

Episode #291

Absolute power does not corrupt absolutely, that's complete bullshit. It magnifies your character.

Episode #695

McDonald's kills more people than war.

Episode #662

[Americans] have been entertained into madness.

Episode #661

Get to a point where you can't be tricked.

Episode #658

Poor is a state of mind.

Episode #661

That's the problem with postmodernism. There's nothing . . . the art is people buying it. The art is the art of control, and it's fascinating to watch. You'll put a little dot on a piece of paper, and you'll use all this [propaganda] to make people see value in it. It's fascinating. That's the art, the art is in the distribution . . . It's about compliance art. It's the art of war. The art of subversion.

Art Before the Horse special, 36:40

People instinctively show you what they are all the time. And it takes real cowardice to get to a point where you don't see it anymore.

Episode #272

I've accepted that it's up to me to discern.

Episode #749

A river can't own water. It just flows.

Episode #572

In the land of the blind, the man with one eye is king.

Episode #530

Depression is regret of the past; anxiety is anticipation of the future.

You can't pin evil on a demographic. You just can't. And it's such a crutch that I see people doing.

Episode #667

Until people speak honestly, they can't even begin to help themselves.

Episode #762 (bonus)

When I'm making fun of a demographic, I don't hate them.

Episode #247

Cognitive dissonance makes you slow.

Episode #230

It's true on every level . . . it doesn't have to be one or the other.

Episode #729

We're all on the spectrum. That's what a spectrum is.

Episode #680

It's the accepted hypocrisy. It's the constant state of contradiction that I have a problem with. Because we're all hypocrites, but it's unintentional. We don't intentionally live a life of hypocrisy.

Episode #301

The majority of people doing bad things are simply operating on bad information.

Episode #724

You can pretend that pipes made out of paper will be adequate, but it won't be, and then you'll drown in your own shit.

Episode #695

CHAPTER 4

Value of Discomfort

Most people would rather buy a car than reinvent the wheel. It's one of those platitudes that's so obvious no one ever bothers talking about it. So I will. At first glance, the choice between what's easy and what's difficult is a no-brainer. What's the value in spending your entire life monkeying around with a transistor if your laptop runs just fine? If someone has already put in the work to build a helpful tool, you may as well make use of it. You could always just build something else. There's always more to do. While we're at it, why grow food when you can go to the supermarket? Who doesn't like things to be just a little bit easier? A little more comfortable? I know I'm not about to reinvent computers. It's beyond my skillset, and besides, I'd much rather just write this book. As human beings in the twenty-first century, it's become second nature to pragmatically enjoy our lofty unearned perches. Whether it's acquiring the currency of time, the currency of money, or the currency of knowledge, our pattern of behavior is the same: We leverage the sweat equity of our long line of predecessors for the acquisition of *more*.

However, as with every virtue, the vice is built in. Being big lacks being small. Being rigid lacks being fluid. Being complex lacks being simple. In our preference for the virtue of shortcuts and ease, we travel a smooth path lined with the vice of a few tempting dangers: the atrophy of chronic comfort, the laziness of groupthink, and the vulnerability of dependence. Mainstream culture is a construction project the size of forever, placed in a finite medium. This never-ending algorithm of our advancement has become a parody: a cartoonish skyscraper leaning fore and aft in the threatening wind. Like the Tower of Babel, eventually the whole thing starts to teeter under its own weight, optimistically overshooting its capacity to scale. Utilizing the tools forged in the hearth of others' sweat equity, we risk a kind of supreme comfort that concludes with a violation of the basic tenets of God's moral law. As human beings, we're not built for this secular concrete jungle. We're built to contend with nature.[17] But what's nature?

I'll be candid. Nature is a bitch. She's beautiful, life-giving, and filled with purpose. But Hell hath no fury . . . If you're weak, soft, or slow to adapt, nature will eat you up and spit you out without a second thought. In order to contend with nature, you have to be tough. You have to compete with every unforgiving damnable thing around you: wild plants, wilder animals, and the ruthless icy cold or stifling fiery heat of the very air you breathe. As a consequence, we became fundamentally wired to overcome the torturous challenges of a psychotically vicious environment. It was the only way to survive. We adapted to battle against discomfort, against hardship, and against pain.

I'll spare you the suspense: We won the long war. However, we've got a new problem. Ironically, man's beat-down victory against nature and our corresponding graduation from the food chain as human beings has produced a new kind of meta-predator: the despair of our own minds. Our inherent need to contend with something has been so successful that we've managed to overstep

---

[17]   This is one of those discernment moments; the degree to which we're built for nature is up for debate. We don't seem to be made for nature in the same way that animals are made for nature.

our bounds. We've pushed against the forces of our fluid medium and swum upwards with such force that we shot right out the top. Now we're fish out of water lying on a synthetic beach of our own creation, wondering why it hurts to breathe.

Our nature is to be close to nature. Smartphones and Snapchat don't cut it. We swapped up the environment, and what worked well in one context isn't working well in another. As human beings, we're optimized for something that is not this. Depression is up. Despair is up. Suicide is up. It's not a mystery why. We conflated *easier* with *better* and overshot the mark. Like a seed, we require the friction of discomfort to thrive. The proclivity to embrace a fight only works well in an environment where there's something to fight against. Because of our modern material overshoot, we've created dissonance: Our environment is at odds with our nature. We're told to relax and take it easy, but we thrive with the task of the grind. We're beasts of burden with nothing to do, rightfully disgusted with our own idle, soft hands. The quiet cry of the modern man is from the pain of indulgence, the pain from a lack of challenge, the pain from a lack of pain.

Now more than ever, whole generations of young men have been utterly removed from any sort of respectable hero's journey. The smooth silk of modernity is bought and sold for its softness. People wrap themselves against the cold of anxiety in a blanket of lazy indulgence, brainless entertainment, and porn. Like a drug addict, our culture's elected solution to our rampant cortisol has been to scarf down buckets of dopamine. We traded a real life with struggle for a synthetic one with chemical crutches. As living men and women, we're sinking into the sensory deprivation tanks of our own neglect of nature.

What a bizarre phenomenon. Without the appropriate context, "Lack of discomfort creates discomfort" sounds like a paradox. Apply some discernment, however, and it makes all the sense in the world. My education in the valuable lessons of discomfort first came to me in the temple of athletics. Pound your feet on a glorious red oval, whose rubber heart beats a magnificent lifeblood of grit and conviction, and you'll know what it means to be alive. You could learn everything you need to know as a serious athlete. In hindsight, running is one of those enigmas that's difficult to explain. It's like how every successful adult knows what it is to have a deep desire to pass profound knowledge on to a younger generation but fails to find the words that adequately explains a feeling. "Work hard and, uh . . . don't do drugs" just seems to fall a little flat. How can an old-timer sum up the transcendent feeling of a whole lifetime of thriving for their uncompromising conviction in a few words? They can't. Part of the human experience means learning hard lessons, but you never quite get there without the direct exposure that comes with moving your own two feet. Learn to train hard and you'll learn to live well. "No pain, no gain" is the credo for a fulfilling life for a reason.

As long as we're on the topic, I see a lot of confusion in the domain of fitness and health, specifically when it comes to exercise and calories. People think that it costs a lot of calories to move. It's not true. The high-calorie cost of training is in the recovery. For example, when David Rudisha set the world record in the 800 meters, it cost him about 100 calories during the race itself. That's one banana. He crushed one of the most phenomenal athletic performances of all time but only burned a fraction of the calories that are in one of those faggoccinos at your gay little coffee shop. (*How dare you say faggoccino.*) Over the next few days, Rudisha's body spent thousands of calories to repair all the physiological damage. Think of it like building a house: It's easy to knock out a wall, but it's expensive to rebuild. If you want to burn big-time calories, you gotta break some stuff. High intensity exercise burns a high number of calories, just not in the moment. Like any other elite athlete with a long history of hard training, I've become capable of prompting my body to burn, say, two thousand calories as a result of two minutes of exercise, but only if I'm willing to embrace some serious discomfort now and reap the benefits from it later.

What's interesting about the athlete's brutal cycle of training is how fundamental the fractal pattern is. Look for the cycle of stress adaptation and you'll find it everywhere. Super-compensation is the resting pulse of our physiology. I'll explain. Since the body has no way of predicting the future, it needs an input to know what to do. Exercise itself is an input; the process of doing damage to break down your body is a specific indication of what should be improved. In this process of adaptation, opportunity cost is the limiting factor. Where should valuable resources be spent? A strong body? A strong mind? Neither? Both? It all depends on how rigorously these things are being used. Why pay for something you won't benefit from? Everything has a cost, and in the world of resource-scarce competition, efficiency is king. A race car is more expensive than a commuter because of the relationship between performance and price. The more specialized something is, the more resource-intensive it becomes. You can run like a cheetah or fly like a hawk, but you can't do both. You can jump like a gazelle or climb like a monkey, but you can't do both. You can have the powerful brain of a human or survive without food for months, but you can't do both. Performance has costs that get exponentially more expensive with specialization.

Fair enough, but where does pain and discomfort factor into all of this? It's not exactly a good time. What's the physiological usefulness of hurting? When I first asked myself this question, I thought I was on the steep precipice of embarking on a long and arduous philosophical journey for the ages! But no. My very next thought was the immediate, obvious answer: Pain is a deterrent. Simple as that. No epic philosophical saga necessary. Pain is the negative emotional stick to positive emotions' carrot. In running, for example, pain keeps a woman from trotting along until she breaks, dead from muscle tears and bone fractures. It's fun to go fast, but it's less fun to die of dehydration because you lacked the discomfort to slow down and seek water. Anywhere you put it, unchecked power is a disaster of an algorithm.

Consequently, discomfort functions as a test. Your physiology is always asking you questions: How much do you really want it? How important is your performance at this? Okay, how about *that?* Enough to overcome pain? If you make the decision to push through discomfort, you just communicated something to your body: "We need to spend resources to be better at this." No pain, no gain is the fundamental algorithm. Want to be faster? Embrace discomfort and run hard. Want to be emotionally tougher? Embrace discomfort and have the fight. Want to be smarter? Embrace discomfort and engage with painful thoughts that challenge your paradigm. Learning to think well is just like being a good athlete: the process of improvement is exhausting. Embracing discomfort is just an inevitable part of the process. Every area of performance can be improved with a decision to embrace discomfort, because discomfort is where the boundary of competence is. And pushing a boundary requires contact with it.

For the uninitiated, the concept behind why embracing discomfort works can be a revolutionary idea. I've seen the eyes of men twice my age light up in conversations where I talk about what I've written here. It's exciting to learn that you can fundamentally change the way you think about the discomfort in your life. Most people think of pain as a problem, but it's not. Such a revelation could flip your whole life upside down. It would be like learning that all your garbage was actually gold. Finding your zone of improvement, however, is to aim at shifting goalposts. As you get better at handling discomfort, you'll find you can handle more discomfort. An athlete who wants to keep getting faster needs to keep training harder: more speed, more volume, more practice. But as you build, you'll run into increasing opportunity costs. If you want to be a professional athlete, there's a good chance you'll have to spend all day training. But most people don't want to spend all of their daylight suffering through the increasingly challenging training of a professional athlete. They just want to avoid cancer and look decent in the mirror. They want a balanced life.

Intense pain can pay for itself in remarkable ways. Great men suffer great pain to become who they are. But is it worth it? Owen expressed a similar issue on a livestream: "How do you give your kids ambition without hurting them?" (Episode #717).

This is something any parent can relate to. Big Bear wants his children to become hard-working high achievers like him, but he can't imagine voluntarily putting them through all the intense suffering and childhood abuse that was necessary for him to become such an indomitable workhorse. Essentially, the question boils down to this: How do my kids reap the benefits of suffering without having to suffer? The answer is: they can't. The benefits of discomfort require discomfort. That's inescapable. You don't get one without the other. This is why high-achieving parents often have low-achieving children: they don't want their kids to suffer like they did. However, there's good news: Although discomfort is required for growth and strength, you're free to choose which kind. Not all discomfort is created equally. Some types of discomfort are a joy. Others are horrifying. This is why getting kids involved in sports, for example, is such a godsend. They experience discomfort on a field, where it's fun, rather than at the hands of something predatory, where it's the stuff of nightmares. High-level athletes become high-level achievers in other areas because the algorithm of the discomfort is transferrable. The secret to running fast is that there is no secret, just "trials of miles and miles of trials."[18]

Because our culture is so catastrophically off the mark, this next point is one I hesitate to bring up. However, I'll address the concept since it's technically true: too much discomfort is also a problem. You'll burn out. The virtue-and-vice paradigm of comfort and discomfort is key to unlocking a personal Goldilocks zone. Everyone's got one: not too hot, not too cold. Finding your personally tailored balance is an individual process. Even the most psychotic high achievers need to relax once in a while, if

[18]   Check out John L. Parker's novel *Once a Runner*.

only to crush harder later. What's important to understand is that it's not discomfort itself that's desirable, but the beneficial second-order, third-order, and fifty-ninth-order consequences that require discomfort to manifest as a result. A discerning athlete needs to learn the difference between training discomfort and injury discomfort in order to be successful. A thriving relationship needs both spouses to learn the difference between discomfort that yields growth and discomfort that yields destruction. A successful thinker needs to understand the difference between engaging with uncomfortable ideas versus simply wallowing in the abyss of despair. There're types of discomfort that build, and then there're types of discomfort that break.

To find the balance, I try to be self-aware, and understand the nature of what I'm doing—growth or destruction? I make time for the full cycle of both comfort and discomfort every day. I test my limits and consciously seek discomfort wherever I can in areas that I want to improve: writing, running, and business. But I also make time to relax and recharge. If I'm never challenging myself with discomfort, then I'm letting the atrophy sink in and I'm not improving. If I'm never recovering, then I'm not setting myself up for continued crushing. Finding a balance between the two is in itself an uncomfortable challenge worth embracing. Culturally, the same algorithm applies. Unfortunately, we've accepted the chronic-comfort version of things. Wealth, technology, and corporations have systematized softness. Comfort begets more comfort. The houses are getting bigger. The couches are getting comfier. The pants are getting fancier. All the while a bleak mix of depression and anxiety has been building. This isn't some sort of demonic joke or odd mystery; we've designed a system on the assumption that more comfort is always better. This is wrong. It's a simple case of good logic operating on bad assumptions. Just ask a computer scientist, they get it: "garbage in, garbage out." And our consumerist culture really is trash.

Productive discomfort is no longer an obligation, it's now a choice. Left to our own devices, we volunteer for less productive discomfort than we should. We've made the mistake of believing that we can jettison every form of pain and still have good lives. Most people spend hours sitting on a couch, never learn anything about growing food, and become consumed by their chronic indulgences. Consciously, people think nothing is out of the ordinary here, but our subconscious knows better. Trying to remove all constructive discomfort merely succeeds in creating a void that only destructive discomfort can refill. If your life is too easy, your instincts will tell you something is wrong. And your instincts are right. Anxiety about laziness is appropriate. Are you eating to live or dying to eat? How about your values? What is your relationship with self-ownership? Do you want to go through the trouble of learning why you do things? Is the discomfort worth it? Learning the precise intricacies of the values you wish to aim for is a rabbit hole you could spend the rest of your life diving down. Like in the case of your phone's circuitry, learning something can be an extreme that many people aren't interested in. Whatever area of your life you're not pushing into a zone of discomfort, however, is the area that atrophies. Just like a body, your mind and morals get slow, weak, and sick if you spend hours on the couch watching propaganda, eating poisonous goodies, and abandoning responsibility. A man or woman who isn't spending time investigating his or her values is allowing themselves to atrophy ethically—the proverbial moral couch potato.

If you're not the one taking responsibility for building your own house of values, then your culture will do it for you, with or without your consent. And just like the carbon lump on the couch who doesn't choose what programs are siphoned through the TV (they're all junk), you don't get to choose what values the mainstream advocates. Pragmatically, this would be okay (I guess) in a culture with good morals, but that's a fantasy. It's totally hypothetical. Our culture is run by business and media. Does blindly trusting massive corporations and mainstream media to build your house of values sound like a good idea to you? Poisonous moldy carrots and venomous pointed sticks have no interest in your well-being. None at all. They're not the ones obligated to live in the tacky apartment of consumerism. They're not the ones who feel your cold emptiness of secular nihilism. They're not the ones so depressed and anxious that they'll believe any nonsense pushed by pixels as long as they get their soft validation: "Good puppy dog." For its ease and comfort, men and women have committed to the path of least resistance. The trouble is, it's the same path that leads to misery. Allowing this technocratic corporatocracy to discern on your behalf by trusting in whatever is mainstream is to co-sign the Devil's deal. Soda sales and burger bargains do not care if refined sugar and synthetic fat give you diabetes and cancer. Your misery does not factor into their equation except as an adjacent proxy for the bottom line. Enormous corporations prefer a miserable buyer to a joyous non-buyer eight days a week. To them, you're a statistic. Losing a foot or getting so fat you can't walk helps their profit margins, as long as these places are still wheelchair accessible. And ramps are easy to build.[19]

To close this chapter out, I'll tell you a quick story. Years ago, I was living in Gage Towers as an undergrad at UBC. On paper, I was at school for mining engineering. In reality, I was a student of the 800 meters. After my second run for the day, I was headed for the elevator. As I turned the corner, looking down the long hall to the steel doors, I saw that the girl who lived on the 16th floor with me was already in the heavy contraption, alone. Seeing me, she reached down and pressed the open button as the doors made a move to close. My legs felt achy but I

---

[19]   We're all proud of Big Bear, who has come a long way with his ramp building.

hustled it in, jogging a few big exaggerated steps with an animated face that hinted at a smile. "Thanks J," I said, crossing the threshold. "Of course!" she piped back a bit too enthusiastically. J-dog was a little weird, but fun-weird, y'know? Normally, I'd lead the conversation, but I was feeling a bit fatigued for chatter. Halfway up an awkwardly silent elevator ride she leaned towards me, slowly leading with her nose, and took a big, obvious, audible inhale, with her nostrils two inches from my shoulder. With wide eyes, my head turned, robotic. With a sideways glance and one eyebrow cocked, a question tumbled out. "Did you just . . . *smell* me?" I asked, choking back a laugh with faux incredulousness. She said nothing, caught dead to rights, staring straight ahead, burning a hole in the elevator door. After a few seconds of silence, I just raised my eyebrows. Resigned, I turned my head back to neutral and thought about how I'd poke fun at her about this later. Ending the pause, she suddenly chirped, "What cologne are you wearing? It's really nice!" My mind mechanically charged through a mental checklist: no deodorant, haven't showered today, *definitely* no cologne, scent-free laundry detergent, I don't even own shampoo. *What the hell* is she talking about? In a flash of realization, I couldn't help but let out a sudden deep belly laugh. I put on my best Southern accent. "I ain't wearin' nuthin', gurl. Tha's jus' the smeyll of a man at his crayft! Yezzir, tha's mah odah! Gahd's honest truth." With wide eyes, J-dog let out a surprised high-pitched peep as her hand shot up to cover the O formed by her mouth. She couldn't help laughing as her face went scarlet, evidently embarrassed by her confession of being partial to my unmasked scent.

There's no shortage of people who would question my hygiene on that fateful, funny day in the elevator. And fair enough, I probably could have used a shower that morning. However, some people would push even further, adamant that deodorant is somehow a hygienic must-have. That's where I'll push back. I haven't worn deodorant in what must be close to ten years. It wasn't a big issue for me; one day I just kind of . . . stopped wearing it. The amount of complaints I've had about that? Precisely zero. And my friends certainly wouldn't have a problem telling me I stink. The number of compliments? Well . . . I think just the one. So the score is 1–0. As far as I'm concerned, that's a big win. Back me up here, soccer fans.

Answering J-dog's question about my "cologne" brings up an interesting point about discomfort. Let's put on our discernment hats and do some problem solving. Smelling bad is a problem. But what's a problem composed of? A cause and an effect. So, where does deodorant fit into this equation? It's an *effect-focused* solution. Deodorant has nothing whatsoever to do with what is causing you to smell bad. It doesn't solve the cause of mean stink, it simply covers it up by masking the effect. So what? Where does addressing the cause of smelling bad get us? Under the psycho-physiological hood. In the West, people think that the problem of smelling bad is a trivial issue. That's only half true. You could argue that the effect is trivial, but the underlying cause is most definitely not. Smelling bad is an indication that something is psycho-physiologically wrong. Your nature hasn't gone rogue, it's pointing at a legitimate problem. You might stink because your diet is terrible—that's a real problem. You might stink because you don't exercise enough—that's a real problem. You might stink because you're chronically stressed—that's a real problem.

Let's say you've got a dude who eats junky food. He's not hydrated. He's got a job and lifestyle that gives him chronic stress. His hormones have gone nuclear. He's not socially well adjusted, and he exercises about as much as a bag of potatoes. In other words: your typical college student. Buddy stinks because he's a mess. What does solving his problem of stench look like when done at the causal level? In other words, how do we make our stinky friend here smell good (or at least not awful) without synthetic crutches like deodorant or cologne? You've got to completely revolutionize this man's life! You have to turn an unhealthy man into a healthy one. His diet, his lifestyle, his mind, everything. Top to bottom. Inside and out. Physically and mentally. His problem of smelling bad isn't solved until his totality is oriented in good health, rather than unhealth.[20] That's not a trivial issue. That's the exact opposite of a trivial issue. You have to change everything about this guy. Deodorant is a quick and dirty way to fake good overall health by masking the helpful way in which it expresses itself: as an offensive stench. What's a better solution than pretending to be healthy? Being healthy.

So why doesn't everyone do this? If it's so obviously much better to just ditch deodorant and smell good for your authentic health, what's with the enormous market for these cancer-causing pasty pit sticks? Why do people get the twinge of incredulous anger if you suggest that deodorant is a puzzle piece worth chucking? I'm certain that there's a long and complex answer that you could write a whole book about, using precise discernment to investigate the intricacies of human nature, herd mentality, and the brainwashing of businesses, but there's another answer with a simpler resolution: It's more comfortable to take the path of least resistance. Putting deodorant on takes about three seconds. Solving your social anxiety could take ten years. It's a shame that people take the easy path, however, because how comfortable something is is a poor measure of its value.

---

[20] Sometimes a man will smell bad to a woman because they're a poor genetic match in terms of offspring. Not much to be done about that.

I'm not advocating that people walk around offending noses. I'm recommending that people do something more authentic about solving the problem. Taking the hard path is the road to better rewards. The lessons of life that are kept from us are done so for the discomfort that withholds them. People avoid switching jobs because its inconvenient, but doing so could save your marriage. People avoid exercise because its uncomfortable, but doing so could save your life. People avoid the discomfort of an honorable existence because civil moral degeneracy is convenient. The values of our contemporary culture, however, have proved to be a disaster. We've made the mistake of outsourcing our discomfort to our own detriment.

It's the easiest thing in the world to float down the path of least resistance, but our choice to do so has literally made us stink. Our health is in jeopardy. Our outlook is in despair. Our culture is in shambles. The good news is that any human being—anywhere, at any time—can get off the train. We can change our mindsets and embrace discomfort, rather than reject it. Our non-helpful negative emotion that's been culturally building stems from a failure to acknowledge our own nature as beasts of burden. When we choose to seek comfort only, we invite horror upon our own souls. Learning to thrive means learning to voluntarily inhabit environments that test us. Every electrical engineer is obligated to take the time to learn the challenging fundamentals of electromagnetism. Every healthy marriage is obligated to make the effort to work through the uncomfortable parts. Every living man or woman interested in achieving a fulfilling life is obligated to make the conscious choice to embrace the value of discomfort. If nothing else, the journey of finding accomplishment in overcoming the challenge of discomfort is gratifying for its authenticity. In this modern world, you have the wonderful gift of agency over your life in ways that would fill the ghosts of history with either envy or adoration. If competence, growth, and strength are goals of yours, then the path to achieving your aspirations is clear: Make the conscientious choice to embrace the value of discomfort. But you'll need some courage to do it.

We're all standing on shoulders of giants.

Episode #725

My life's been such a beautiful tragedy . . .
I have the best life in the world, and just
constant abuse.

Episode #809

There's no better feeling that doing labor
on your own land.

Episode #290

So many good people don't have the fortune of having just so much awful stuff thrown at them.

Episode #753 (bonus)

Take a warrior man, a man genetically designed to protect, and you give him no mission; that's death to society.

I think people are drowning in empathy and alleviation of pain.

Episode #814, 9:38

There's nothing wrong with pain. Pain is growth. I'm comfortable with pain now.

Episode #264

You get stronger the more you fight.

Episode #827, 2:32:15

Sometimes obstacles are what allow you to get to the next level. And there's always going to be obstacles.

Episode #727

The amount of creativity that comes from pain is unbelievable.

Simple is the hardest thing to do.

Without evil or suffering, you can't become strong.

Episode #724

People are a process. We're all a process. We're all growing and learning. And the people that I recommend you keep close to you, which is what I've always done, are the people that understand your process . . .

Episode #261

If you're happy all the time, you're not trying hard enough.

Really reconnect to your ancestors . . . it's tough living in a world of plenty when you come from a place of extreme scarcity.

Episode #802, 31:54

That's reality . . . Whatever you suppress comes back with a vengeance. That's why you gotta work through shit. And be honest with yourself about your problems, because, if not, it'll come back in a fiery fucked up way.

Episode #288

I think I kind of like crazy people a little bit.

Episode #293

You gotta address your weaknesses in order to beat them.

Episode #280

Every testing is a blessing.

The more you can understand and deal with pain, the more beautiful your life will be.

Episode #815, 1:25:23

It's just nauseating . . . the people that act [so fearful], do you smell? What's your stench like?

More discomfort quotes:

Until you take personal responsibility for the temptations, you're part of that cycle and all you're doing is hurting yourself.

Sometimes the best thing to happen to you is some really bad shit.

Profit that's unearned makes a dead soul.

Episode #207

If you're not excited about that much sleep, you're not working hard enough.

Moon Anniversary stream

It's not easy to communicate with people that want to be angry.

Episode #1028, April 15

And another part of my awakening, I think, has been caring about you guys. Every day spending a few hours focusing on what matters . . . I think the curse of the messenger and the blessing of the messenger is pretty profound . . . the curse of the messenger is you are forever an outcast. The blessing of the messenger is the love you have for the message and who you're bringing it to and for the future is so mind-blowingly profound that you grow. And you see more.

Episode #1028, April 15

Guilt is good . . . when your soul screams, "Don't feed your kids poison," listen.

Episode #661

If you have logos, it's all a blessing. All of it. Every disaster that hits you is a freedom . . . they're burning dead wood.

Episode #809

CHAPTER 5

Value of Courage

You know what panic feels like. You know the rush of cortisol that hits like a train, chemically obliterating your insides with the brutal fury of a red-eyed steely demon. You know the feeling of tension, when your heart thumps in your ears. A different part of your personality takes over. You become jumpy and skittish. Like a prey animal, something deeply instinctual writhes in hysteria. *Get out! Get out! Get out!* Your clammy hands might shake. Your vision might narrow. Your chest might be left breathless, desperately fighting for air against the pressure of panic. Sometimes the terror can come in a flash, forming a pit in your stomach. A stumble on a treacherous cliff. A surge of panic about your child's life. A cold brush with death on the highway.

Fear is such a debilitating, uncomfortable emotion that many people are simply unwilling to confront it in all its forms. At the time of this writing (mid-March 2020), carunka virus is sweeping the world . . . says the news. From my perspective, all I see is a pandemic of fear, people who have watched too many episodes of *The Walking Dead* reacting to more pixels on a screen. Human beings are drowning in cortisol dumps because they aren't willing to embrace the discomfort of honest discernment. Everywhere, people who trust their screens are saying the same thing: "No one I know is in a hospital, dying of something the news is screeching about . . . but I *know* it's super-bad out there!"[21] When this first started, I met a lady who said her uncle died of coroh-no: he was also eighty-three (which is a year older than average life expectancy in Canada), smoked, had asthma, was obese, *and* had caught pneumonia on a cruise ship . . . but it was the 'roner that got him. I'm just going to back away slowly. Just smile and nod. Fear is a virus.

---

[21] Upon revisions several months later, I can make the same claim. So much for the twelve-day incubation nonsense.

I was reminded of this when I went to Costco the other day. The first wave of empty shelves at department stores had just happened a few days prior, and people were feeling the twinge of panic after being unable to buy exactly what they wanted—for the first time ever. A few days later, after the store managers adjusted and stocked up, the shelves managed to keep up to the demand just fine. I watched from the wings as a forklift moved pallet after pallet after pallet of toilet paper back and forth. Two little ladies operating as mousey bouncers behind a collapsible yellow barrier were restricting consumers to a mere hundred double rolls. In the aisles, pallets of food were spilling out into the lanes everywhere, exceeding the hysterical demand to stack cans filled with sorbitol, xanthate, and sodium bi-gluti-something (or whatever the hell) to the ceiling.

I passed by a lady, whom I'll call Pam, whose cart was revealing. Her archetypal fear pile was a perfect fractal representation of what was happening at the larger scale. Panicked for her health, Pam (amazingly) stacked her cart with unhealthy food, an enormous pile of cancer-causing junk squirreled away for tomorrow. Predictably, Pam's loaded buggy also hosted the Costco store limit of toilet paper hoarded up in a great billowing fortress of kaolinite and dead carbon. But I guess enough ass tissues for a small army wasn't enough, so she also threw on a gargantuan pack of paper towels. What's mystifying is even that wasn't enough, so she topped it off with none other than what might go down in history as the least-flattering panic purchase on God's green earth: adult diapers. In her prey-like panic, she was quite literally preparing to shit herself.[22]

Pam's lesbian hair (cut short and dyed a tired crimson) spoke to what I can only guess is her worldview—stereotypical, modern progressivism. It might not come as a surprise, then, when I tell you that Pam's health was waning. Pam had the physique of a wilting onion; she was bulbous and sickly looking. (*How dare you.*) Her unwell, drained complexion engulfed a pair of dark cloudy eyes, sunken into her puffy face. I could see her consternation when I glanced into her murky pools of despair. Pam had the look of a scared rabbit bleeding from its head, staining the hair color that God intended. Her startled, reactionary movements in the world spoke to her perspective of it: a great predator. I could see her ungrounded, panic-stricken soul bouncing around inside like a ping-pong ball getting smacked so hard it was ready to pop. Pam was afraid. She was flooded with fear because the news told her to be fearful, and she wasn't well because her habits made her unwell. Pam was hurting herself. Her choices turned her into a serious risk for every sickness under the sun: cancer, diabetes, fatty liver disease, heart disease,

---

[22] Pam wasn't buying for her elderly parents, either. That day, there was a Pam-type cart in every direction: toilet paper limit, paper towel limit and adult diapers. These people were preparing for an a-poo-calypse.

gallstones, osteoarthritis, gout, sleep apnea, stroke, cancer, hypertension, hormone imbalance, mental health issues . . . the list goes on, and on, and on, and on, and on, the privilege of extravagant indulgence.

But is Pam at least enjoying her indulgences? Of course not! Her quality of life is terrible. She's miserable for her lack of embraced discomfort. Pam hates that she lives like a jittery drug addict, hooked on huge dumps of dopamine, always scrounging up whatever she can get, always on edge. Her body—aiming for homeostasis—has adjusted to the truckloads of dopamine by building up a tolerance to it. Pam doesn't enjoy the simple things anymore. Her fear-oriented neurotransmitters have been highjacked by material secularism. The delayed little drips of dopamine that come from reading, studying, or self-reflection just don't do it for her these days, so she bails on these habits altogether. To overcome her cortisol, she needs the immediate fat smack of dopamine to feel any positivity at all: refined sugar, TV, and social media. BAM. BAM. BAM. Without the courage to embrace good values, Pam's habits took her down to a level of degeneracy that ravaged her body, mind, and soul.

One of Pam's most destructive habits is consuming the news. Every time she tunes in, the TV hits her with a poignant dose of trauma. Fear this, fear that, fear him, fear her, but above all, really don't forget to be afraid. Like the swine flu, the bird flu, or the Zika virus, the Bogeyman's gon' getcha'. And just like every other time, "this time it's different". Coming from the same people waving the fear flag about weapons of mass destruction, rising sea levels, or the impending unavoidable horror of . . . quicksand, let's just say I have my doubts.[23] Pam's cage is so rattled that she's too afraid to get up and check the unlocked door herself. She's free except in the place where it counts: her own mind. Hypnotized by the petrifying circus on her screen, she sits fearfully still, grateful to gobble down the poison she's been fed: the junky "food" of the corporatocracy engine, the worldview of the mainstream news, and the dodgy habits of a reactionary prey animal, never thinking ahead. She has internalized hysteria. Pam, like many others, is shocked into just going with the flow, floating down the endless lazy river of an anesthetized human experience, hooked on a prescription of indulgence that promises sweet relief from anxiety and fear. The same demons peddling the "solution" are also the ones creating the problem.

It's awful that such a thing happens. It should be a priority for men and women to elevate each other out of these fear-based pits of tragedy. I'm not talking about charity. I'm talking about making a real effort to forge

---

[23] So . . . about that whole New-York-will-be-underwater-by-2015 thing . . . Does anybody who watches the news have a memory that dates back as far as the distant long-before times of 2008? It'd be good to heal the amnesia now and stop trusting proven liars.

values. There's strength in building. Teach a man to fish, so to speak. This gift of life is begging to be a wonderful celebration of all things good, beautiful, and true. With such a staggering opportunity, it's imperative that we understand why fruitful lives have become rotten for so many. It's imperative to understand fear.

Watch enough super-scary stuff on the TV, and it becomes rooted in the subconscious, especially for the people who don't realize what's happening. Consumers have been petrified into submission. They're terrified of social ostracism. Contemporary mentality is herd mentality. Modern life is to get along. Never say anything too true or discerning as to ruffle any feathers. This causal chain all comes back to the same anchor points: fear of loss, fear of damage, fear of discomfort. In a brutal, ironic twist of reality, Pam finds herself in pain for her fear of pain. Her addiction to the cortisol hits of the news have her in a hysteria, mindlessly sprinting toward what's actually killing her: box after box of synthetic poison disguised as food for its predatory dopamine hits, a gluttonous tower piled up in shameful indifference for authentic health in a Costco cart. Pam's fear of death is killing her.

This all may sound a little "doom and gloom," but there's good news! A solution is always nearby. The value of courage can strengthen human beings to overcome fear and follow good principles. Find courage and you can be honest. Find courage and you can discern. Find courage and you can embrace discomfort. It's courage that empowers human beings to choose principles over dopamine dumps. Our courage to speak honestly and transparently is necessary for our empowerment: piecing together the proverbial elephant of the greater truth. For its fearfulness, the morality of modern secular consciousness has been manufactured completely upside down. With a bit of courage, we can flip it back again.

This isn't just a thought experiment. Take a gander at Big Bear's life and you'll see a rare tangible example of what acting with courage in the modern public sphere looks like. It takes real courage to maintain your principles when the stakes are high. In order to honestly voice his criticism against the push for trans children, Owen had to risk his name and hold the line when that hypothetical fear became a tangible reality. Every reasonable man or woman agrees that chemically castrating a three-year-old is child abuse, but the progressivist gatekeepers that rule Hollywood will kick you out if you say so. For his decision to speak up, the name of Owen Benjamin was blacklisted. After years of building a successful career as a comedian, it was as if someone flicked a switch and the whole game changed overnight. Owen got booted out of Hollywood. He thought he was done. In some ways, he was. Clubs wouldn't book him. He couldn't even rent independent venues. Owen wasn't allowed to step foot in the Hollywood Improv—he was denied entry into the same building that painted his face on the outside of its walls for all the success he had within them.

Big Bear's podcast, *Why Didn't They Laugh*, is a years-long example of what honest thinking looks like. The whole thing is a fascinating stream of consciousness. By adapting to new information, Owen's entire worldview has incrementally changed. He doesn't get stuck in a loop, endlessly repeating himself like other social influencers too afraid of the unknown to branch out. To be willing to flip your whole internal world upside down if necessary requires courage. Owen adapts and moves on, maintaining his basic principles. Selling out isn't in his blood. Moral values have a cost that the Big Bear is forever happy to pay. In the demographic of public influencers, this is the exception rather than the rule. As the most popular influencers gain money or clout, they become too averse to losing it, and won't honestly adapt to new information. They let the clicks guide their words, never moving on. The anti-government guys rant endlessly about the utopia of anarcho-capitalism. The conservatives rant endlessly about the left, putting everything in a political lens. The fear-porn salesmen spiral endlessly to turn a profit, selling everything from emergency food packs to boner pills. These people turn their names into a brand. Like a corporation, or corpus, or non-living thing, they sell people the worldview they want, packaged just the way they want it: spineless.

Courage generates better rewards than money. Although currencies can be partially exchanged, truth, discernment, and discomfort aren't the same thing as cash, social approval, or clicks. If you're ascending, sooner or later you'll just have to make your choice: truth acquisition or power acquisition. The best at one must be willing to sacrifice the other. Although our culture has become unbearable for its fearfulness, we're finding our way back to courage again. Logos is rising as some legends might say.[24] With such elevating turbulence, it feels like something is stirring. When your only choices are waking up to hard truths or living a nightmare, people start to open their eyes. But this groggy awakening is happening slowly, incrementally. The value of courage, like any other value, builds on itself gradually. Show just a little bit of courage in your day and you'll find that you're able to show a little more the next. You have to test, and push, and build, to improve. Do that for a year and see what happens. The news says the Apocalypse is coming. Great! Fine by me. If prime-time anchors think that everybody is going to be afraid of whatever comes next, I've got some news: "apocalypse" just means "revelation," or "great unveiling." If you're an honorable living man or woman, the unmasking of the world's secrets is the best thing that could possibly happen for you. Just don't be afraid, and what's next will be a blessing, I promise. A great revelation is taking place, and the people who can find the value

---

[24]   Check out E. Michael Jones who has produced plenty of content discussing the profound idea of the word logos. It is truth, the word, and logic incarnate.

of courage to embrace it and push open the unlocked cage are having the best time. If I was afraid of the social pushback, then this book (as well as the two to follow in this trilogy I have planned) would never have been written. Looking forward, the value to come next operates on the same continuous trajectory as the values before it; there is a logical progression to investigating these ideas. Successfully speaking out against the purported status quo like Owen has done, and I hope to do, inevitably generates conflict, which is why doing so, is a man's job. (*How dare you.*)

> There's a fine line between righteous indignation and panic.

Episode #848, 24:15

> If you act out of emotion, you're most likely wrong.

Episode #172

> This is the best time to be alive I can possibly imagine if you're not scared.

Episode #753

It's like being around five-year-olds all day . . . they literally wear adult diapers.

Episode #988, March 22, 2020

Fear kills. *Right now.*

Episode #767

How do you function? How do you do anything that's valuable to anyone with the fear you have?

Episode #771 (bonus)

If it's always hindsight, you haven't learned yet. You haven't learned that fear is the weapon.

Episode #754

Fear is the enemy. Never forget that.

Episode #653

I'm so sick of cowards. I got a homestead, I make a fine living, I bring a lot of quality to people's lives, it's not going anywhere, I have no fear, I'm fired up because I'm sick of watching the dead bury the dead when I think they might have a pulse.

Episode #767

You don't require people to save you when you aren't afraid.

Episode #788

I've lived thirty-nine years, I'm a controversial figure. I've pissed off a lot of really powerful people. I've never seen the inside of a jail or a gulag in my life. What I've seen is fear. What I've seen is carrots and sticks that make people not want to have children. That's the genocide.

Episode #715

I fell out of hell, and on the way out I thought I met people that were good, and they weren't.

Episode #705

As a man, you have to give peace and strength to your family and community. Fear is the worst.

Episode #767

More courage quotes:

When you're in that culture of fear, you can't make anything good.

Episode #273

It's almost too hard to fathom that some people are just that cowardly . . . 30 percent of the country acts like someone has a gun to their head.

Episode # 273

Don't run from a predator or they'll instinctively jump on you.

Episode #723

Real heroes? You don't even know their name. The hero is a good role model. You don't even know their name.

Fear is the only way to make a good man do bad things.

Episode #753

The fear is the weapon.

Episode # 664

Don't be scared.

I didn't feel fear or despair. It would be much worse to bend my knee.

Fear is from the enemy. Always.

Episode #666

How do you function? How do you do anything that's valuable to anyone with the fear you have?

Episode #771 (bonus)

Are you scared? Are you a special-boy? Are you begging someone to take the pain away?

Episode #770

The fear is a reflection of your own mind.

Episode #777

The fearful hate the fearless.

Episode #786

Your fear is self-inflicted.

Episode #784

The downside of [having] a really low fear response is sometimes I have to keep myself in check that I don't just keep putting myself in crazy situations 'cause I know how productive it is. I'm sure some of you guys relate to it. I don't mind being in front of a charging rhino. In fact, I think subconsciously I find myself gravitating toward danger because I know how productive it is. When I'm broke, I do my best writing. When I'm kicked off a platform . . . I inspire the best . . . that's when I crush the hardest, and so, oddly, that's what I have to watch out for: [that I] don't just keep poking rhinos for no reason.

Episode #814, 43:20

I don't get humiliated by [social ridicule] because I don't put any value in the opinion of cowards.

Episode #234

How dare you not be afraid? How dare you not be scared all the time?

Episode #988, March 22

Any fear is a sign of extreme weakness.

Episode #755

Are you going to be afraid because of the media? You failed.

CHAPTER 6

Value of Masculinity

Toxic masculinity! Men harm society! Bigoted, evil, sexist, cis-gendered, heteronormative patriarchy! What a mammoth load of crap. Academia is infested. The university culture is a completely homogenized, soft, sensitive goo of limp-wristed, pearl-clutching, nannying nonsense machines. (*How dare you.*) Superfluous alliteration aside, it's no surprise that for men everywhere, school was hell. Sitting down in a chronically feminized environment, being forced to endlessly comply in a delicate, competition-free zone is horribly deflating for the male psyche. Men want to compete! Men want a challenge! Men want to crush! Put the damn grades next to the names so I can kick Jimmy's ass! I don't care about his stupid feelings. If he can't handle second place, that's a him-issue; Jimmy needs to find some courage, embrace discomfort, and toughen up. Be better Jimmy, be better. Why in sweet icy hell would a young boy bother studying without a social incentive when he can just lie to his parents about his homework and play video games? I remember being that kid: hating school, rejecting my teachers, and lying about my responsibilities. I hadn't worked through the value of honesty myself yet and was too stubborn to listen to the advice from others about it. In class, "Because I said so" wasn't exactly the most compelling thing in the world coming from Ms. Fergy-bergy, a thin-haired, abusive old bag sipping a questionable yellow drink (definitely urine) every Friday with a grimace, *waay* too fat to get her Costco-sized caboose up the stairs.[25] What a time to be alive.

Before we dive into the value of masculinity, I feel obligated to do a bit of tedious housework and frame the conversation. It feels like posturing against the arguments

---

[25]   She used the elevator. As for the whole urine drinking situation? I dunno, man. But that was urine, I'd bet Jimmy's life on it.

of ghosts, but that's okay, it's good discernment practice. Here we go . . . Gender is a different category than gender traits. Men and women are defined by their chromosomes, whereas masculine and feminine are defined by general traits of the group. Bit of a yawn-fest, I know. However, it's important to understand that they're completely different resolutions. When I mention something that is masculine, I'm referring to general traits of men as a group. Like being tall, women can exhibit these traits too. A woman isn't any less of a woman if she exhibits masculine traits, because her chromosomes didn't magically change; what's feminine is a different category than what's female. My buddy Gertrude[26] is an enormous, strong, gruff, hairy, loud woman. She's masculine as all hell, but 100 percent woman. If Gertrude's feelings are hurt by the reality that she's a masculine woman, that isn't a valid reason to demolish a useful category that accurately describes reality, it's just an unwelcome opportunity to benefit from the process of finding the courage to embrace discomfort and discern what's true. If Gertrude can be honest about what she is—a woman—and what traits she exhibits—masculine ones—and still find confidence and self-respect despite not fitting into a more desirable mold, then she becomes a force to be reckoned with. Gertrude crushes

---

[26] I don't actually have a friend named Gertrude, but if I did, she'd be a crusher. No SJW nonsense from my ol' buddy Gertrude.

for the power of her authenticity. Pretending that the term *feminine* has no legitimate definition is a quick path to spending an entire life in a low-vibration state of anxiety induced by self-deception. Being a masculine man or a feminine woman is what you might call an ideal. Being imperfect isn't an excuse to start redefining terms into ludicrous oblivion. Reasonable, courageous, discerning, honest human beings definitely do not throw the baby out with the bathwater. Deconstructionist (baby-chucking) thinking isn't helpful here, or anywhere else, which is why academia is cannibalizing itself. Even as a college graduate, I'm more than fine with the institution's self-destruction.[27] An organization that puts the youth in debt, lies about everything, and hates masculinity wholesale? Good riddance.

The keen observer might notice that in this book, there is no "value of femininity" chapter to balance out the value of masculinity. (*How dare you.*) Is this because I don't believe there's value in femininity? Of course not. It just doesn't need yet another voice. The value of femininity is preached everywhere you go. The whole culture is overtly feminized well past the point of being tyrannical. Right now, the culture definitely doesn't need yet another voice evangelizing softness, sympathy, or an endless shrill callout for the poor, helpless downtrodden. Caring for

---

[27]   Technically I graduated with a B.Eng from the University of British Columbia, but I just like the word "college."

others instead of encouraging them to learn to take care of themselves has become a supreme mainstream cultural value. Compassion has overtaken conscientiousness at all kinds of cultural resolutions, even at the level of legislation, where it's a catastrophic failure. Tolerance isn't a virtue for its own sake. Masculine values like intolerance desperately need more authentic voices now. So, here we are.

With that in mind, what is masculinity? What anchors the totality of masculinity as one non-nebulous thing? When you think about the most high-octane form of masculinity, what comes to mind? Superhero? Race-car driver? Drug kingpin? Bear-wrestler? World conqueror on horseback? Shredding a guitar solo to "Seven Nation Army" with bloody fingers? Riding a tiger with two rifles on a mountaintop, surrounded by fireworks as an angelic soundtrack of a thousand gorgeous women sing your legendary name that *echoes across eternity!?* No? Okay, I'll put you down as a maybe.

To sort out this mystery of defining masculinity, we'll walk through a quick example . . . in nature! Consider the difference between a male and female deer. The big distinction that jumps out at you is the antlers on the male's head. Now, I'm not really the type to question why one might have weapons sticking out of one's head, as the undeniable badassery of it all is obviously enough justification, but let's get a little crazy here and do it anyway. What's the purpose of Duran the deer's cranial billy clubs? Why bother with the fight? *Can't we all just get along?!* The answer is an unambiguous, uncompromising, and most definitive, no. When it comes to deer disputes, there's a prominent reward for victory, and therefore a serious incentive to invest in good armament for the bout. For the individual bucks, when they step into the ring to smash racks, they know full well that it's the winner who gets to breed. The reason the females agree to be enablers in this process—other than because it's awesome—is because a trial by combat is both an effective and efficient way to outsource the task of sorting out who has the strongest genes. As we've discussed, nature is a bitch, and survival of the fittest really matters when you haven't graduated from the food chain. Free from any real hardship, the mainstream culture has developed concerns revolving around the rotund: survival of the fattest. In college, "woke" progressives consider themselves cutting edge, focused on dull ideas as pathetic as microaggressions, as insane as gender fluidity, or as retarded as language policing. (*How dare you.*) No complaints about toxic heteronormative behavior from the fuzzy four-legged ladies in brown, however; they know better than your average college sophomore. The animal kingdom has a lot more sense than such vomit-inducing curricula as English 206: A history of gendered language. *Barf.* In the deer hierarchy, where concerns about triggers have more to do with flying bullets than flying words, showcasing your strength, power, and speed as the strongest physical specimen is the route to propagating genetics. The stress test for masculinity is conflict.

What's important to understand here is that the conflict itself is a necessary condition for the improvements found in the value of discomfort. If the bucks weren't fighting as individuals, they wouldn't be improving as a species. This thought experiment about Bambi and her macho head-butting compadres is enlightening. What defines the beating heart of masculinity is a willingness for conflict. Look at any of the stereotypes for masculine behavior among men and you'll find that this concept of embracing conflict holds. Every masculine archetype, from the superhero to the warlord, is notably stalwart in his commitment to embracing conflict, because the vehicle of conflict functions as the fundamental delivery system for strength and competence. This fractal pattern is everywhere. Masculine conflict between ideas and perspectives provides more truth and discernment. Masculine conflict against a grimy workday provides a better livelihood and more competence. Masculine conflict against feared predators and tyrants provides safety and freedom.

Why is a man considered more masculine if he shows competence at overcoming the challenge of his craft? Because he's proven himself to be the stronger deer. It's just a more sophisticated version of the same pattern. The value of overcoming a challenge need not be limited to brute force, because as human beings we can afford to value both brains and brawn (not to mention a litany of other values). Our efficiency, cooperation, and graduation from the food chain has transcended the need to be exclusively reliant on physicality for survival. All the same, we would be remiss to overlook the value of masculinity—which is exactly what our culture is currently doing. Look around. It isn't hard to see that the enormously valuable conflict-seeking philosophy of masculinity has been deliberately suppressed. What's happened to young boys in school is a catastrophe. We're killing them safely. There is a whole generation of men who grew up without sufficient exposure to conflict and discomfort. Grown men are crying—literally crying—for safe spaces, more indulgence, and their government to save them with more "rights." These feminized men and manically cartoonish women throw tantrums, screeching about nonsense they haven't bothered to try being honest about, let alone taking the next step to discern. At the cultural level, the tyrannical side of the feminine nature has expressed itself as a soft twisted flower, through which its ideologically tempting nectar has crippled young boys.

Blue-haired feminists want to talk systemic sexism? No problem. How about a school system that tells boys their God-given nature is inherently toxic?[28] How about a deliberate attempt to beat the toughness out of boys until they're malleable, compliant little tax donkeys? How

---

[28]   Corohno closing down schools is a blessing.

about a culture that aims for its men to be so weak-willed that they won't even say what they know to be true? A downvote on social media? Heaven forbid. At the cultural level, the male psyche been tested and it has failed. Men didn't offer enough pushback for their principles. They didn't stand up for the value of masculinity, or anything else for that matter. In hindsight, we can learn from these past mistakes. We can realize the utility of conflict. Time to be a little more honest and put the grades back on display.[29] On this point, what grade would men give their own morals? Are you watching porn there, Jimmy-Jim? Then ya failed a test, bud. Be better Jimmy. Be better. The ethical answer is to fight the gluttonous, hedonic, weaponized indulgences that create fragile, polluted, conflict-avoidant minds.

Something important to understand is that this criticism isn't a complaint. It's a call to action. Do better in your own life. Be tougher. Have values. Men who complain about this scenario of cultural unfairness and immediately put themselves in a victim class so they can appeal to some form of a higher authority are, ironically, failing to exhibit the masculinity necessary to get out of this mess in the first place. Masculine men don't complain. They act. In the face of conflict, an honorable, masculine man simply

---

[29] Homeschooling would be even better.

smiles when he says, "Conflict is the air we breathe. It's the water in which we swim."[30]

To refuse victim status, then, is the responsibility of the masculine. Masculinity and victimhood are mutually exclusive. These perspectives cannot coexist. You must choose one or the other. Masculine philosophy is a strength-based philosophy: taking personal accountability for rising up to the conflicts of your life. Victimhood is simply resignation, shying away from the conflict. Is a militant mouth breather yelling at you about putting a diaper on your face? You're no victim—learn common law. Is a tyrannical school system jeopardizing your children's ability to have a discerning mind? You're no victim—start homeschooling. Is a tyrannical politician growing your government like a cancerous wart? You're no victim—start a homestead. This masculine, anti-victim philosophy is especially helpful for times when things could otherwise feel overwhelming. Although it's easy to point at elements in your life that you have no control over, the fact is, how those elements affect you does fall within your control. Oddly enough, the willingness to embrace conflict can open up an opportunity for stoicism.

To embrace masculinity is to believe that being a victim is a state of mind that can be rejected, that victimhood is inherently a choice, not a circumstance. A

---

[30]   A quote from the venerable legend himself, Vox Day. Check out his blog: Voxday.blogspot.com

battle is only over when you agree to stop fighting. Losing in a conflict or feeling pain doesn't categorize you as a victim by default. This is just an opportunity to learn and improve by way of a test for whatever comes next. Ask the right question and any conflict can be a little quiz. Many theists believe that all of life is simply a test of the soul by God. This staggeringly powerful idea is something even the lonely atheist can benefit from (albeit a much lesser version) if they're masculine enough. All it takes is to ask the right question yourself. Find the courage to just say the words "can I beat this?" and you're set. It doesn't matter how difficult the circumstance. Asking the question immediately changes the nature of the pain or the challenge, transcending it from meaningless discomfort that beats you down to meaningful discomfort that builds you up, because it just became a test of your courage, resilience, and strength. Damn, that's manly.

Conflict can always be an authentic learning experience if it's aimed at a genuine goal. One of the differences between the blind men who can argue and figure out what an elephant is and the blind men who just kill each other in stupidity is their perspective of their conflict. What is the intent behind the conflict? Is the conflict sourced as a vehicle for getting somewhere better, like the truth, or is the conflict a manifestation of a deep insecurity that feels personally attacked? Is a man's aggression his way of self-soothing with anger, or is his passion behind the conflict just basic masculinity seeking greener pastures? There is a difference. Not all conflict is created equal. We fight with our words so we don't have to kill each other.

What's critical to understand is that honorable masculine men embrace conflict from an ethical place. Good conflict is very productive. Viewing all conflict as bad conflict is the error of the tyrannical feminine or the gamma male.[31] He can't take a joke, let alone a punch to the face. It's like the difference between wrestling wolves and a panicked prey animal: one is happy to be scrappy while the other thinks that it's about to die any time he sees teeth. Eternally fearful, weak men lash out in panic at the first sign of strength. They're not fun to be around for their condescending sarcasm, cynicism, and peevishness. When it comes to the discernment surrounding masculinity, understanding the purpose of conflict, as well as when and where to apply it, is the key to the whole thing.

In truth, honorable men embrace the value of conflict because we like it. Whether it's socially, athletically, or intellectually, masculine men relish the opportunity to compete as an enjoyable inevitability of life. However, our conflict also conveniently functions as something useful in the culture: a delivery system that actively improves the human experience. It's a crooked trick that our "leaders" have pulled off, convincing the mainstream culture that

---

[31]   Search "gamma" on voxday.blogspot.com for an in-depth analysis.

conflict is somehow innately immoral. In public school, feminine finger wagging is about all the encouragement that teachers have to offer for the youthful modern male. This isn't an argument that says women are bad. They're not. Like literally everything else in this world, femininity has a downside. I'm arguing that the feminine nature doesn't work well for everything. It doesn't scale well. What works for nurturing babies doesn't work for forging grown men, and by extension a successful culture. Put through this meat tenderizer of modern feminine culture, wild, competitive boys have come out as soft, cordial "men" incapable of doing their jobs. However, the masculine nature isn't broken nationwide. Honorable men still exist, none of whom consider themselves victims of anything. Instead, when honorable men see a problem, they simply feel purpose in the fight against it. They build rather than beg. There's an army of masculine men content to clash in the culture war like Owen Benjamin. We're happy to headbutt the challenge into oblivion. Such stubbornness is something that many women and feminine men don't understand. "Just say different words—why fight when you can get along?" Because it's what we do. It's how we thrive. At the end of the day, it's in our nature. Can you really blame us for seeking to fight for honorable values like freedom?

> Public school was designed to make slaves.

Let's try and figure it out without yelling at each other.

I'm just a window into a normal dude struggling honestly, and I think that's what draws people to the stream . . . is just how not special I am.

Episode #278

This fear people have of confrontation is fucking crazy. It's a failure of the masculine.

Episode #787

You fight the monsters and then you get to live your nice life.

[In] toxic femininity, the sins of envy and greed come out hard, and in toxic masculinity, the sins of rage and lust.

Episode #200

Stand for nothing, fall for anything.

Episode #548

The best way to resist tyranny is to refuse to be a victim.

You fight with your eyes open every day of your life, and then you die.

Episode #539

This is clearly a test. It's a place to get stronger.

Episode #784

Violence comes from the white knuckles of quiet desperation.

Episode #651

It's exciting! We can prove ourselves. We can fight again.

Other people will become much happier people if you don't let them walk all over you. I promise. It's a gift. If you keep your kids in line, If you keep everyone around you in line—not control, not do-as-I-say-without-any-logic—but if you put boundaries around you and you make disrespecting you expensive, or not respecting the rules of the situation, they get happier. It's the opposite of what people think intuitively because of our messed-up culture. People think that if you allow others to walk all over you, and you just are nice and passive and tolerant, you're somehow doing them a favor. You're killing them.

Episode #1026

More masculinity quotes:

The character of the man says everything.

It's straight-up warfare what I'm doing right now.

Episode #262

A lot of hatred is a soothing mechanism.

Episode #800, 56:09

It's funny how when I call out abuse, people freak out . . . it's because when you're an abuser—and I'm not saying

131

pedophile—but just, you pray on the weak at some point in your life; if someone calls that out, like what I'm doing right now, it makes you furious. And you then hate me for it, because you know what you are.

Episode #301

It doesn't take a mathematician to watch the algorithm play out. If you do not either try to take the weapon from your enemy, or you use the same weapon, [you're going to lose].

Episode #295

The normal strategies of dividing only work when the men are weak.

Episode #677

Start nothing, finish everything.

Episode #688

I get the tingle of rebellion when people don't tell me their rules.

Episode #686

Who do you think is coming to get you?
Your conscience?"

Episode #213

You can tell what a man values by how he
mocks you.

At what point do you say no [regardless]
of the consequences?

Episode #542

We don't need to raise hell. Hell is being
raised.

It's a tough pill to swallow, but unless you
do, you're not really fighting. You're not
really fighting unless you face it. Because
you're just roleplaying that you give a shit.

It's conflict management, not conflict
resolution.

Let the Devil kill you and watch him
disappear.

Once you take a knee you don't stand back up.

The fact that they went to war at all means that both sides lost.

Why do these people seem incapable of resisting war?

Episode #666

While you're proving them wrong, you're living a great life.

I have been silenced for saying what [others] believe secretly.

Why didn't anyone say anything?

War is tough to judge . . . I'll go to war if I have to. Never want it. It's like trying to set fire to your neighbor in an apartment complex—it's going to burn you too.

Do you not know how land is acquired? How nations are built? All of it is on blood. Blood and steel.

Episode #299

Someone has to want something in order to get it.

Episode #186

Life is just scraping barnacles.

We're going to kick you out of a prison.

I was willing to fall.

It's harder now.

Ego will get you killed . . . if you can't readjust your perspective, you're going to die.

The passage of time is abuse.

The only thing new is the pace of change.

Episode #172

There's no going back, because it doesn't exist the way it used to.

Episode #211

I've lived a conversation I've never had.

Episode #546

Enjoy how it makes you feel. The pain. That's a monster I'm killing.

Strength. Truth. Work. Family. They can't touch ya.

The wicked flee when no one pursueth.

Episode #705

Just because it hurts doesn't mean it's not true.

Episode #703

Wanna know what makes someone a hero sometimes? . . . the ability to take the boos.

Episode #290

All the people that are the most angry are the ones that realize they could have and didn't . . . when people say I don't have anything to prove, I know. But I also do have to fight for what's mine.

Episode #715

Unless you understand evil, you can't fight it.

Episode #660

I figured out a lot of life through some of these pitfalls.

Episode #232

That's the beauty. Darkness can reenergize you... it can refocus you.

Episode #657

We lose everything if we just start making it so people have to think a certain way.

Episode #272

You know you're over the target when people can't stand up to reality.

Episode #691

Our battles aren't flesh and blood. It's principalities and darkness.

Episode #763

Bad men are dead men walking.

Engaging in your sorrow and your victim narratives does nothing.

Episode #708

You're the one who did it. Granted, I may have inspired, but that's the role of men.

Episode #727

I like producers. I can't stand destroyers.

Episode #275

You're a killer who hasn't killed yet.

Episode #266

Huge success and huge loss is a little window into someone's soul... when the chips are down is when you really see the character of a man.

Episode #687

It's one catastrophe at a time right now.

Episode #226

This isn't a place for victims.

Don't complain and comply.

Episode #713

Don't act like you don't know something and allow yourself to be controlled by demons that are on television.

Episode #765

[Confrontation] is all it takes, guy. All it takes is to not sit.

Some people avoid conflict. I love it.

May 3, 1:29:36

By the way, they're about to fight with swords. All people these days have to do is walk into a grocery store without a fucking mask on. It's insane how the stakes have changed.

April 24, 1:29:36

I don't get scared, I get focused.

Episode #206

I'm not here to lose... I was an underdog and now I'm not.

Episode #700

If you crumble at my words, you deserve to crumble.

Episode #658

This is what I do. I fight. I'm a fighter.

Episode #673

CHAPTER 7

Value of Freedom

"SAAAAAFETYYYYYY!!!!" That's what Wilma Wallace—William Wallace's imaginary female counterpart—would have belted out in her last triumphant moments of life before being gutted by the oligarchs of the day. But social movements need not always follow their demographic archetypes. Rewind your wristwatch a few decades and you'll find a few women's marches that took on a contrasting tone from their modern dainty goosestep. Because universities mandated campus curfews for women—on the grounds that rape took place almost exclusively at night—the women embraced their masculine sides and fought back. Like William, they cried for FREEEEDOMMMM!!! They made their demands clear: "Give us the freedom to risk rape." A few decades later, the repercussions of hookup culture have been endured, causing the pendulum to swing back: women are not happy with what's going on. The supposed "freedom" of sexual liberation is not exactly jiving with feminine nature.[32] (*How dare you.*) Consequently, Wilma has taken back the reins. Suffice it so say, she's upset. For the first time in recent history, a social movement is demanding less freedom, not more. Feeling unsafe, college harpies have demanded their institutions step-to and "just, like, uh"—I'll translate here—"legislate morality already." They've effectively outsourced the responsibility of providing safety from their individual masculine friends and partners to their enormous, and growing, governing bodies. Women cried out, turning to their institutions for protection, because their men failed to provide it themselves.

What does safety look like at the institutional level? How does it actually operate? For universities, anti-rape regulations meant setting curfews for women, keeping them safe from the hazards of mixing hormones with Hennessy. But why is this the go-to strategy? Why

---

[32]   Which we'll investigate more in chapter 10.

does a governing body set a rule where the majority suffers for the benefit of the minority? Why look after the lowest common denominator? Why make rules for the exception? It's because although the overwhelming majority of women at parties don't get raped, some of them do. If it's the university's responsibility for setting up rules that protect everybody, including the minority, don't be surprised when a ten p.m. curfew gets put in place, even it if doesn't work well. It's just a basic numbers game. Enormous numbers of people × small chance of a lot of awful = a lot of awful happening to a lot of people. For this reason, legislation is not an effective solution for many problems. Yet it's the option many people are clamoring for, because they refuse to take personal accountability. When the responsibility of high-stakes consequences for a large group of people falls to the law, then the politicians' hands are tied. Everyone must drive the speed limit. Nobody gets to party. They have no choice but to restrict freedom for the good of all humans. At least, that's the civil narrative, assuming benevolent political leaders. A laughable mischaracterization.

To investigate the value of freedom, a good place to start is by looking at a situation with an archetypal lack of freedom. Being a marginally literate person, the first place my mind goes is to the much referenced, quasi-fictional dystopia described in Aldous Huxley's masterwork *Brave New World*, wherein ten world controllers make the decision to leverage indulgence as the control mechanism for power. These world controllers give the tax/labor cattle (the people) all the sex and drugs they want in exchange for their liberty.[33] The tax donkeys in *Brave New World* take the ticket and submit to the state. Floating down their lazy river of indulgence, they simply consume without purpose, void of honesty, discernment, discomfort, courage, masculinity, or autonomy. Is any of this starting to sound familiar? What's so interesting about *Brave New World* is how readers respond: they have difficulty articulating what causes the unsettling sense of foreboding in the text. Despite the obvious tyranny in *Brave New World*, readers can't articulate what's so awful about what's going on: exchanging freedom for indulgence. Ask the average college dude-bro what the problem is with culturally accepted, constant, easy access to all the sex he wants, and you'll often get an answer that's about as sophisticated as an episode of *The Retarded Housewives of Florida Trash* (*how dare you*): "Uhhhhh . . . like, uhh . . ." Why would a young man, raised exclusively on the value of chronic civil comforts, be able to articulate the problems with it? Bombarded by the relentlessness of mainstream media, he's been pulverized with the endless blitzkrieg message of indulgence: *casual sex has no downsides, casual*

---

[33]   Check out E. Michael Jones's work *Libido Dominandi* for more on how sexual liberation is the lynchpin of modern tyrannical control from the oligarchs of our time.

sex has no downsides, casual sex has no downsides. Now Jimmy, what are the downsides of casual sex? "Uhhhh . . ."

Part of this problem, then, is the issue of manufactured consent. Spend your entire life being told to pursue something and you're much more likely to "choose" to do so. "No downsides to speak of when it comes to indulgence," says the mainstream narrative through thin, greased lips to their fat, sick tax donkeys. The people who design the public-school system (that teachers are obligated to enforce) deliberately lie while skulking away from anything useful. What a bunch of lizards. Show of hands, how many people from the city were taught the Socratic method growing up?[34] Okay . . . how money works?[35] How to grow food?[36] Any basic life skills? Anyone? *Anyone?* Now, how many people were taught that college is a good

---

[34] The Socratic method is a dialogue that takes the form of cooperative argument with the intent of determining truth. Basically, just logical back and forth questions between people who aren't getting angry with each other.

[35] Money is mostly debt which is "formed" as a function of interest rates, backed by nothing. It operates on a model that requires continuous exponential growth (like a Ponzi scheme—hint, hint). Money is based on the promise of future labor. Fractional lending is insane. Derivatives are nuts. Think of it like a Jenga tower on meth. The taller it gets . . .

[36] Potato goes in the dirt. I've been informed by a Russian correspondent that some North American's think potatoes grow on trees. They uh . . . don't.

investment? Or that the Bible is filled with pernicious lies? Or that Southerners are a bunch of low-IQ, slave-seeking rednecks? In public school, what's empowering is demonized, and what's demonic is empowered. Believe it or not, the cutting-edge curriculum in US public schools teaches everything from anal sex and bloodplay to embracing your gayness with trans demon storytelling. Progressivism is . . . progressing. Forcing the kids of undiscerning and emotionally unavailable parents out of those environments because of the carunku virus has been a blessing as far as anyone honorable is concerned.

Despite such manufactured ideas in mainstream civil culture, human beings always have their core nature. We can always come back. Owen's growing audience is. I did. Even years of this conditioning doesn't entirely crush the soul. Instinctually, readers of *Brave New World* can sense the truth of its wickedness even if they can't articulate why. Every kind of institutional tyranny, even the ones that leverage indulgences, are fundamentally wretched. The "cheap" indulgences of life come at a very serious cost. Being starved of discomfort would be awful, because discomfort brings value. Aha! So lacking discomfort is a problem in *Brave New World*. But is a lack of discomfort the fundamental source of wretchedness pervading Huxley's not-so-distant dystopia? Maybe not. Consider the flip side of the authoritarian coin: George Orwell's classic, *1984*. Unlike Huxley's world, the inhabitants of Oceania are decidedly *not* comfortable. They're exhausted, dreary, and, on the whole, miserable. This tyranny is much more in-your-face. Big Brother rules without the twerking fishhook of offered indulgences. He is not a crook tradesman selling the ol' bait and switch, but a master hypnotist and bully. His craft is submission, not compliance. How many fingers, Winston? Wrong answer, Winston. How many fingers, Winston? *Wrong answer, Winston.* It's all pain and misery. Fear and hopelessness. Rather than turning minds into mush, like the velvet oligarchs of *Brave New World*, Big Brother prefers to grind them into sand. He smashes rather than smothers his people. Instead of being pulled by their greed, the suppressed souls of Oceania are pushed by their fear. Instead of hounding for the carrot, they're beaten with the stick. Although the methods for locomotion differ, the direction of movement is the same. It's all for tyrannical control. A lack of self-determination. Compliance for the sake of compliance. A distinct *lack* of freedom.

One effect of this deficit of freedom is the tyrant's miscalibration for your life. An oligarch in control doesn't know—and frankly doesn't care—about you personally. Another factor for this miscalibration is our inevitable variance as people. As shown in *1984*, Winston, with his lung problems, does not enjoy his morning exercise. In that same environment, however, an elite athlete would walk away from such a paltry routine still ravenous for more. No set of habits is perfect for everyone. The consequences of lacking freedom, however, descend far beneath the lifestyle it spawns, be it the vacuous degeneracy of *Brave New World* or the venomous viper pit of *1984*. Lacking freedom is a catastrophe regardless of how it is brought about because the value of freedom is what provides an authentic human experience. The deluge of depressed determinists out there saturated in the indulgence of modernity isn't a coincidence; free choice is the genesis of transcendent meaning.

Authentic choice is all that separates consent from manufactured consent. The hellscape of *Brave New World* demonstrates this perfectly. The citizens of this dystopia, much like our own civilization, overlook the manufactured element of their consent. Porn? Give it to me. Drugs? Dope. Cheesecake? Sweet. The motto for modernity is complaisant: "don't mind if I do". The lynchpin that secures this machine of unacknowledged enslavement is that it feels good to indulge. People do more than just fall in line. They beg for it. Unaware of the nature of their hedonic treadmills, the eternally indulgent endlessly chase gluttonous vices as the anxiety builds in tandem with their appetites.

So, you could say this isn't ideal. We can do better. The value of freedom is something to aim for. Autonomy is something to seek. A destination to move toward. But what is freedom? What does it really mean, precisely, to be free? Who's free? Who's not free? How do you know whether your consent is manufactured or authentic? The idea of "freedom" *feels* obvious, but try putting it into words. Like the details of any abstraction, it's surprisingly complex at a high enough resolution. What specific questions about freedom prompt an effective answer? How can you tell if you're thinking freely? How can you tell if you're acting freely? Where's the line? How thick is that line? How transparent? My motivation for investigating aspects of both *Brave New World* and *1984* isn't to argue that the sky is falling down or that the government is about to kick in your door, but simply to get an archetypal sense of what freedom isn't, which can help us discern, reverse-engineer, and finally define what it is. In both of these sickening dystopias, the slimy oligarchs in charge focus on the control of people. They're obsessed with restraining the thoughts and actions of those they wish to rule. Freedom, then, is about will. It's all about being unrestrained. The astute reader now might think, *But there are always restraints!* the Socratic response to which gets us headed in the right direction.

I'd like to offer two distinct terms: a *boundary* and a *restraint*. The boundary is the outer perimeter. It's a border you are not free to move across—a limitation of a kind. Within this boundary is where restraints operate. Think of it like swimming in a pool. The pool wall is a boundary within which you are free to swim, unrestrained in any direction you wish to move. How this concept scales is where things get tricky. How small does a pool have to be before you consider the walls—its boundary—to be a restraint, stealing from you the freedom to swim where you want? One person feels free lounging in a hot tub, while another feels caged in anything smaller than the open ocean. Regardless of how big something gets, the existence of its boundary does not disappear. Everything in this material realm has a boundary. There will always be an outer limit that prevents your free motion at some point. Pick any pond you want, you can't swim in any one direction forever, even in the Atlantic. However, freedom isn't a binary issue. It's an issue of context and discernment. There's a big difference between the *boundary* of a shoreline thousands of miles away and the *restraint* of an anchor around your waist. Both can prevent you from swimming in a hypothetical sense, but the context of how matters. Boundaries don't immediately invalidate the concept of freedom by default, because boundaries can exist outside the area where you desire to make your free choices. In a sense, it's a pragmatic distinction. Your free choice exists within an outer boundary that you're not free to cross. Freedom is willful movement within a volume.

In terms of the mind, being free to think doesn't mean you're free to think *any* thought, because your brain has limitations. Your thoughts can only get as complex as the materially imposed boundary will allow. Being a free thinker isn't defined by a lack of limits. Being a free thinker is defined for a lack of restraints within them. How many of your thoughts are manufactured? How much of the space within your mind is restrained? Weaponized indulgences are rampant now, anchors tied to the swimmer. There's no shortage of Huxley-esque restraints in contemporary life: addictions, vices, debts—you name it. A young man addicted to pornos is not free. He's submitted his will to the restraint of narcissistic indulgence. A college graduate with student debt (like myself) is not free. He's restrained by economic chains that limit his ability to take risks (like writing a book).[37] A news addict who constantly tunes into mindless drivel under the self-soothing guise of "being informed" is not free. She's restrained by an addiction to cortisol. A secret-king keyboard warrior ranting on message boards about his manufactured political opinion is not free. He's restrained by an addiction to outrage. A young woman, convinced by teachers and media that "corporate work is freedom and freedom is slavery," is not free. Her restrained decision to cope with the unfulfilling lifestyle of Brave New America by indulging in drugs and sex with strangers is a product of manufactured consent.

One of the arguments I see is this dichotomy about consciousness. The theists and atheists are locked in a dispute about the reality of our minds; do we have free will or is it all a predetermined material illusion? Being a proponent of free will means that my opponents have a question I need to answer: How can free will and manufactured consent exist simultaneously? Such a duality seems like a paradox. Through discernment however, I contend that it is not. The true answer need not require

---

[37]   I guess I'm not very risk averse.

100 percent free will or 100 percent determinism. Reality is rarely bimodal; nuance is just difficult to understand intuitively. What people want (a simple answer) has nothing to do with what is (a complex reality). While it's true that your mind always has a degree of restraint imposed on it via manufactured consent, which limits your freedom, it's also true that you still have the ability to think freely if you choose to make the extra effort required to do so. This idea is crucial to understand: You're not standing on level ground where every direction is as equally easy to travel as another (perfect freedom), but neither are you plummeting from the heavens, where down is inevitable (perfect determinism). You're standing in the middle of a hill. The restraints of your mind are discouraging you from ascension. The good news is that you have the freedom to do so anyway. Modernity offers the easy way down. It's you who must make the choice to step up. No one is coming to kick in your door. If you let the government tell you what to do, it's because you're consenting to what they're offering. There are restraints that encourage you to be dishonest, undiscerning, chronically comfortable, fearful, and conflict-avoidant, but, in spite of that, you can always embrace the more difficult direction. You can always elevate yourself. You can always choose to be honest. You can always choose to be more discerning. You can always choose to embrace discomfort. You can always choose to find courage. You can always choose to embrace conflict, and can always choose to reject the restraint of

your manufactured consent. You always have the choice of your free will, even if it requires an uphill fight. A man with a gun to his head still has a choice, even if the test on his soul is an extreme one.

Like all of the honorable values I'm advocating for, pursuing the value of freedom doesn't come easy. For example, modern civilized readers, having bought into mainstream dogma, will bristle at my criticisms of feminism. They'll feel a knee-jerk, tribalistic, negative response against an authentic criticism about the destructive lifestyle that has been manufactured for modern women. If this is the case for you, then your beliefs might not be as free as you think they are. Men and women aren't the same. That's a fact. For their differences, what men enjoy most and what women enjoy most aren't the same because what's optimal for what's different, is, of course, different. What to do about that difference at a cultural level is reserved for chapter 10. You're obviously free to disagree when you get there, and I genuinely welcome any well thought out emails if you do.[38] I suppose the trolls can email me too. If you believe that shoving women into cubicles and unpayable debt is the best path toward a great life, then tell me why. I'm all ears and happy to tango. That being said, the point I'm making now isn't actually about any specific belief, but rather to recognize how you got there. I'm discussing the context

---

[38]   TellingJacob33@gmail.com

of the movement, not the destination. Have you really thought your beliefs through, or are you just going with the flow? It's not my job to tell you where or how to swim. I don't care if you're at the bottom of the pool, enjoying the silence of the depths. I care if you're down there because someone strapped an anvil to your back and you haven't realized that you're about to drown.

What path did you take to get where you are? Be honest about the context—was it restrained with lazy, undiscerning, spoon-fed thinking? Do you believe things just because you're told to? For most people, the answer is yes. This is an exercise in self-awareness: Have you thought your beliefs through and genuinely considered dissenting positions, or are they manufactured ideas? Do honest questions about your belief system make you angry? Giant red flag. A free-thinking person can have the conversation without morphing into a screeching tomato, bleating out the songs of their people: ode de crazy, sonnet de social justice, or, most unbearably, the great ballad of the odious white night. How well you handle criticisms of what you believe is a good litmus test for how authentic your path was in getting there. Self-awareness, and recognizing the difference between passion versus rage, is crucial. These days, I still get fired up all the time, but I don't get angry about ideas like I used to; I learned to free my mind through the pursuit of truth, discernment, and a few other values you could probably guess at this point. Now my passion is positive. Strong masculine conversations can embrace conflicting ideas and enjoy the electric energy of it just fine. In contrast, indoctrinated belief systems squirm under scrutiny, desperately lashing out to avoid the pain of confronting unacknowledged subconscious restraints.

Owen cracked the dam of this real-world matrix of manufactured consent when he first turned upstream against the Hollywood narrative. For years, this bear amongst the salmon thought he was just having a good time: crushing performances on stage, touring with the best, and meeting every kind of celebrity. In the raging fluid of Los Angeles (currently stagnant), you're free to swim all you want, as long as you keep in line and descend toward clown hell: hallowed progressivism, degenerate consumption, and dogmatic atheism. Stand up against chemically castrating children, abortion, or gun confiscation, and you're out. By cutting his own strings, Owen inadvertently cut his own funding. It turns out that the two strands of social restraints and money were one and the same. All his doors to income as a comedian slammed shut and he was literally out in the woods, chopping trees to chip away at credit card debt.[39] The illusion of benevolent leadership becomes apparent when you choose to wade up the hill, rather than drift down into the lackadaisical mouth of Hell. Far enough downstream, the demon troll with free floaties and fuzzy navels underneath the sparkly bridge of LGBT+ is encouraging the languid path

---

[39]   It was more like hauling brush as a grounds guy, but I'm a sucker for alluring alliteration. ¯_(ツ)_/¯

toward pedo-ville. Algorithmically, it's where that journey of progressivism inevitably ends. The "+" includes pedophiles by the way—you know, monsters that literally want to have sex with children. In the eyes of "civilized" people, that's the protected class now: vampires hoping to abolish the age of consent, and drain the life force out of kids. If you haven't seen it yet, it's because you aren't looking. And that's not even a criticism, necessarily. It just might not be your role. At this point, though, you either understand the difference between criticizing a group versus attacking an individual or you don't. No one needs to claim a badge of protection because they have a gay friend named Larry in order to criticize a political/social movement that has actively promoted sex with children. Knowing the difference is kryptonite against the feeble SJW backlash of "*how dare you!*" Social shame is just a tool like any other. Some use it to empower others with principles and diligence. Others tyrannically weaponize it as a restraint.

To drive everything home, I'd like to close with an analysis of a biblical story about the value of freedom for its own sake. Since it's so short—twenty-one lines—I'll include the whole thing. This is a translation from the New American Standard Bible.

Luke 15

11 And He said, "A man had two sons. The younger of them said to his father,

'Father, give me the share of the estate that falls to me.' So he divided his wealth between them. And not many days later, the younger son gathered everything together and went on a journey into a distant country, and there he squandered his estate with loose living. Now when he had spent everything, a severe famine occurred in that country, and he began to be impoverished. So he went and hired himself out to one of the citizens of that country, and he sent him into his fields to feed swine. And he would have gladly filled his stomach with the pods that the swine were eating, and no one was giving *anything* to him. But when he came to his senses, he said, 'How many of my father's hired men have more than enough bread, but I am dying here with hunger! I will get up and go to my father, and will say to him, "Father, I have sinned against heaven, and in your sight; I am no longer worthy to be called your son; make me as one of your hired men."' So he got up and came to his father. But while he was still a long way off, his father saw him and felt compassion *for him,* and ran and embraced him and kissed him. And the son said to him, 'Father, I have sinned against heaven and in your sight; I am no longer worthy to be called your son.' But the father said to his slaves, 'Quickly bring out the best robe and put it on him, and put a ring on his hand and sandals on his feet; and bring the fattened calf, kill it, and let us eat and celebrate; for this son of mine was dead and has come to life again; he was lost and has been found.' And they began to celebrate. Now his older son was in the field, and when he came and approached the house, he heard music and dancing. And he summoned one of the servants and *began* inquiring what these things could be. And he said to him, 'Your brother has come, and your father has killed the fatted calf because he has received him back safe and sound.' But he became angry and was not willing to go in; and his father came out and *began* pleading with him. But he answered and said to his father, 'Look! For so many years I have been serving you and I have never neglected a command of yours; and *yet* you have never given me a young goat, so that I might celebrate with my friends; but when this son of yours came, who has devoured your wealth with prostitutes, you killed the fattened calf for him.' And he said to him, 'Son, you have always been with me, and all that is mine is yours. 'But we had to celebrate and rejoice, for this brother of yours was dead and *has begun* to live, and *was* lost and has been found.'"

Profound.

I don't know about you, but for me this story hits like a truck. And not a bitty rice-burner, either. I'm talking V8, V10—big-boy stuff. Like the typical millennial, starved of transcendent horsepower, I spent ten years hobbling on a crutch of indulgence through despondency and atheism. I limped through a world that wasn't the one that my parents would have chosen for me but accommodated all the same. I was a high school kid pulled downhill by the carrot promised in mainstream programming. In hindsight, it's like I couldn't see the world properly, something I think a lot of living men and women can relate to. Like a hazy movie, it was made depressing for its scripted fraudulence. Materialism is a hell of a philosophy. Taking the next step down to determinism is much worse, especially for youth. I played video games religiously, completely addicted. I never watched porn until a guest speaker at high school came in to talk about how "everyone does it."

Why miss out? I thought, with at least ten years of brain development still to go. Everyone said that a life of conspicuous consumption was what I was supposed to do. Now, with a better perspective of our cultural landscape, I count my blessings and reject the hedonic message of modernity. Indulgence isn't something to aspire to, but freedom is. I was lucky to have a reason—athletics—to embrace discomfort and seek strength, which generated the momentum necessary for a journey to finding even more honorable values.

Upon hindsight of my erroneous ways, an unsettling thought materialized: Where were my parents through all this? Why hadn't they forced me to make better decisions in high school, or even college? Why did my first-rate parents let me make third-rate decisions? Because they understood the value of freedom. A forced decision is not a decision at all. They knew their son was suffering, and after some appeals to reason they let it happen, because it needed to be me who had to learn the lessons firsthand. It sounds cruel, or even careless, but it's neither. If I hadn't gone through these trying experiences myself, I would have resented my parents for their force and would have dove down those paths even farther. It's just part of human nature. If my parents had been well-meaning tyrants, then whatever good principles they had tried to force on me would have been tainted in my mind as a representation of my willingness to comply. I never would have learned. I never would have seen the importance of values for their own sake. Instinctually, my parents knew that. By permitting me mistakes, everybody won . . . eventually.

It was a sluggish process, leisurely descending the hill, before genuinely discerning that down was not where I wanted to be. Ultimately, I made the independent choice to march back up and keep marching. If I had been pushed up the hill, beaten by the stick of fear against my own will, then the momentum equation would have been reversed: I would've turned around and starting sprinting back down at first chance. Regardless of the intent behind the stick, it still registers as a stick.

Although it was all for the best, it was a challenge for everyone. It's hard to imagine how difficult it would be to watch your firstborn child make decisions you know are terrible and have the strength to actively choose not to tyrannically overstep—for years. It's like the father of the prodigal son. He knew the risks of permitting his son the freedom to make the mistake of an indulgent life. He knew his son might be doomed but he let him go anyway, because he knew the alternative was a guaranteed disaster: creating a resentful child, bitter for his father's robbery of his life's autonomy and meaningful authenticity. I can relate. Just like the prodigal son who suffered for his freely chosen indulgence and returned, I've come back too. I should have listened when my dad told me to work hard and ditch the video games, or when my mom told me to find one good woman and avoid the pornos. Now, I make these decisions for myself, with gratitude instead of resentment, knowing that my life is genuine for its own sake. None of that could have happened without the freedom I was given. Luckily, I'm not alone in my growing awareness of honorable values. A shift is taking place culturally. Living men and women everywhere are doing the same things: speaking more honestly, seeking more discernment, embracing more discomfort, finding more courage, and embracing more conflict. It's a determined movement against the restraints of modern indulgence culture. We're aiming for the value of freedom.

To answer the pushback: yes, of course parents should inform their kids and guide them as best they can. That almost goes without saying. The value of freedom isn't an excuse for lazy parenting. Like any other virtue, there's a vice inextricably attached to the value of freedom. Children need guidance. Being left alone and directionless is a problem, especially if the environment they're placed in is opportunistic and predatory. To the disappointment of the cultural cannibals, however, we can always make the willful choice to refuse the path of chronic civil comfort. We can recognize the nature of manufactured consent and reject the restraints that form in our character as a consequence of chronic indulgence. Empowering ourselves with the freedom to make our own decisions with a strong, clear mind is the path toward living with authenticity and fulfillment. The point here isn't to say that every free decision is somehow a good one on its own. I know I've had plenty of bad ideas. Instead, the point is to acknowledge that our choices aren't isolated. They're part of a bigger picture. They feed into each other. The mistakes of today can be the lessons of tomorrow, but only if we have the authentic freedom and mindset to learn from them. It helps to have a laugh or three while we do it, too.

> Show that you're not afraid. Show that you don't take safety over freedom.
>
> Stop seeking salvation in the state.

Episode #726

> America is one of the least free countries in the whole world and people don't even realize it because people associate freedom with indulgence.

Episode #742

> It's a given that American is an awesome country. But we have to self-criticize in order to keep it that way.

Episode #292

> The most expensive thing you'll ever pay for is free, because then they'll take everything.

You have to choose your path, or else the path is irrelevant.

That's the one thing about [the ugly] . . . depictions about dystopia. They're all wrong. That's not how it would look. It would look beautiful. But it would not be.

Episode #784 (bonus)

Freedom in America is only about money because we don't recognize that all freedom comes from morality and discipline. It's upside down.

Episode #742

There's a difference between restraint and cowardice . . . Cowardice is you're too scared to act. That's bad. Self-restraint is you can act but you choose not to because it's not strategic.

Episode #225

Breaking chains is not that hard—you just need pliers and a rock. Breaking your passions is a whole different ball game.

Episode #833, 1:40:55

When you [give up freedom], they don't give it back unless you take it back personally. Not with violence but with will.

Episode #803, 36:07

Men require respect, women require a feeling of safety.

Episode #986, March 21, 2020

The way to really assert your sovereignty is in your mind. We're always going to be slaves to somebody. Be a slave to God and truth.

[Hollywood] is just gilded cages.

Episode #684

Looking back, I don't remember. It's almost like I disappeared for a little while.

I don't trust myself to not go down the lazy warm river of escape.

Episode #263

The world is free and beautiful and growing . . . Psychopaths can't touch a free man.

Episode #800, 32:15

I'm alive, and I will never consent to my own death. Spiritually, physically, emotionally, comedically. All these comedians consented to the death of their own art. They said, "I will remove words from my craft. I will take colors out of my palette. I will take notes out of my piano because of the whims of silly little cunts that allowed others to blacken their eyes for money and lollipops and fancy-pants . . . There is something that separates us from animals. There is. And as tragic as today's death [of my baby alpaca] was, it isn't the death of a child. There is something different about humans. We're natural and not simultaneously . . . We bake in the sun and freeze in the cold. Without a lot of building and foresight and community, we're dead. We're not strong for nature. We're real weak. Except for our logos. Except for our processor that's connected to source.

Episode #832, 40:07

More freedom quotes:

[They] become a slave to their instincts.

I don't internalize the will of my oppressors.

I realized I was surrounded by monsters.

Episode #555

It's only offensive if you're trying to make a statement . . . the removal of freedom is the offensive part.

Episode #299

You know you're not oppressed when you get to kill the jester.

Episode #546

You don't need the world to change. You can change.

They freed me.

Unless you are willing to give up everything, you're not free.

Just because people are making horrible mistakes all around you, doesn't mean you have to.

Don't internalize the sins of others.

Episode #550

Entertainment is the Devil's substitute for joy.

You can't innovate unless you set people free.

Die on your feet instead of living on your knees.

If you apologize for things you know aren't wrong, that apology is just an act of submission.

Apologize when you know you're wrong.

Personal accountability is the blood of life.

The child penalty is only a penalty to those who own you.

Episode #678

Freedom comes at a cost, and that's discipline.

Episode #731

You're not free until you admit you're a slave.

Episode #555

Political correctness is nothing more than submission.

Episode #689

You're developing a survival mechanism for tyranny.

I don't care, I'll never be censored. It's not happening.

Episode #667

The best slaves are the ones who don't even know they're slaves.

Episode #668

[No free man] is easy to predict.

Episode #677

The hardest people to control [have] always been farmers, homesteaders.

Episode #655

The way out of this is to do our own thing.

Episode #233

If you attempt to control the world, you're just revealing your own weakness. Your own fear, your own trauma.

Episode #792

Where's your line? If you don't have a line, you're already a slave and you don't even know it.

Episode #795

What the fuck do you do when you're rich? . . . The freedom is more important.

Episode #832, 16:35

Being approved of [by] the celebrity is like being approved of by the slave.

Episode #740 (bonus)

When you give up logos, you have no agency.

Freedom comes with pain and suffering.

CHAPTER 8

Value of Comedy

What do military vets have in common with Paralympians? Missing limbs and wheely good jokes. (*How dare you.*)

When I was a kid, I was always puzzled when I'd see someone in a wheelchair. They oozed caution. They'd take the ramps slow, frantically break eye contact, and avoid curbs for the boring, prudent descent of proper wheelchair access. They'd even speak softly. I couldn't relate to their timid behavior. I'd always imagine myself in their shoes— or chairs—navigating through life. I wouldn't turn to avoid the curb—I'd go right over it. Full speed ahead, baby. Clunking wheels are the sweet sound of conquered hesitation. I wouldn't be leery on the ramps either—I'd be ripping. Sharp turns are easy if you're not a wuss. Downhill sidewalks? Time to fly. Bored in the halls? Obviously I'd be tipped back, balancing on my wheels, unrestrained by terrified teachers. Their knob-knuckled finger pointing at my occasional wipeouts would be a small speedbump against the momentum of my reckless abandon. They couldn't keep me down. Falling off a wheelchair is probably pretty embarrassing, but the thing about that is: who cares? I'd rather pick myself up off the ground to a few awkward chuckles than live with the kind of passive caution that embarrasses a wet-floor sign. Years later, my childhood whimsy about all things wheelchair-related was validated in a cathartic trip to Peru. In February 2019, I began working as a guide runner with a visually impaired athlete, David Johnson.[40] It's my job to be David's eyes. We race together side by side and I give him commands while keeping him in his lane. That summer, David and I touched down in Lima for the Parapan American Games. Thousands of disabled athletes were concentrated in one village, many of them zipping around in wheelchairs.

---

[40] David and I run the 400-meter event together for Canada. His deteriorating eyesight currently sits at 3 percent field of vision. David holds the T12 400-meter Canadian record.

When I saw dudes hopping off curbs and flying down sidewalks, I knew I'd found my kind of wheelie people.

Before meeting para-athletes, I didn't think much of them. (*How dare you.*) My undiscerning perspective was carelessly defined by my opposition to self-righteous progressives and their masturbatory virtue signaling about the disabled. I have always found new age social justice gremlins to be gross; these pudgy desk jockeys, always on their high horse, endlessly blather on about their "support" for "victims" who they always put on pedestals. These outspoken self-satisfied types are the worst. You can always count on the indefinitely delicate to never actually do anything helpful whilst being endlessly vocal about how moral and virtuous they are. Their behavior is nothing more than one self-soothing line after another. Contrary to their crooning, however, being a victim is just a state of mind. A guy in a wheelchair isn't a victim if he makes that choice. Convincing someone they're a helpless victim is the worst thing you could do for them. Treating disabled people differently—even if different is "better"—is, for many, the biggest part of the problem. Although this idea is something I had already understood intellectually, it wasn't internalized in me until meeting so many para athletes: Disabled people are just human beings with different circumstances, and the responsible ones aren't exactly thrilled with patronizing declarations of how "brave" they are for simply existing. They appreciate getting chummy with goofy self-deprecating jokes, just like anyone with their head on straight.

For my disdain of the virtue signalers and my failure to discern, I saw para-athletes as nothing more than a moderately talented crowd of people that happened to have a disability, giving them an "easy" path to the Olympic village. Such a callous perspective is more common than people would like to admit, especially in circles of elite athletes. The most herculean animals in track and field have vicious standards, and the cutthroat metric for judgement in athletics is—spoiler alert—athleticism. On the sacred oval of blood-red, talent, work ethic, and guts are all that matter. And talent comes first. Since able-body athletics pulls from an enormous talent pool and puts only the very best on television, it's extremely elite (and rife with doping). The trouble with para-athletics is of a different kind: the talent pool is tiny. While the danger of an ocean is the predatory feedback loop, the danger of a fish tank is being alone. Compared to the able-body world, the tally for para-athletes is paltry. Of the few that do exist, their competitions are further watered down by being split up into several categories. Inevitably, the Paralympians that make it just aren't as physically talented as their Olympian counterparts. It's a basic numbers game. On average, if para-athletes weren't disabled, they wouldn't have the same speed, power, and strength as the able-bodied professionals. Consequently, many elite able-body athletes see para-athletes as second rate. Especially the ones who would never admit it.

Elite athletes are peacocks, constantly boasting their flair toward others. For their physicality, they measure themselves as superior, even if they don't admit it because of the social blowback. "How dare you" is a big deterrent for the typical civil citizen. The trouble with this unidimensional perspective of the athlete's value system is its failure to discern. My old perspective of para-athletes missed the point. After getting to know a bunch of para-athletes, I learned all about what they have had to deal with just to get where they are. I developed an enormous and authentic respect for these guys. They have guts like you wouldn't believe. They're tough, remarkable human beings who also happen to be a lot of fun to be around. Judging para-athletes exclusively by their raw athletic talent fails to see what makes them admirable human beings.[41] If you took the adversity that runs in lockstep with being disabled and exposed it to your "typical" elite able-body athlete, it would incinerate them. Like rising ash, they'd spiral into despair, losing their grounding; unable to bear the broiling, feverish sense of fundamental undoing associated with losing a limb, proper motor function, or the ability to see. Not so with para-athletes. Instead, successful para-athletes learn not just to cope, but to thrive in the painful heat. The immense fire

---

[41] I don't want to undersell them too much here either. Many Paralympians are, obviously, exceptional athletes.

that they can manage is what forges such commendable character. In the blaze that threatens suffering, they always find a way to extinguish their own annihilation with a laugh.

In Lima's athlete village, antics were bountiful. Every day we'd start joking when we woke up and wouldn't stop until we were asleep. Disfigured limbs took on names like "Snoopy" or "bear-paw" as they'd flail or wiggle about to the chuckles of others at a café table. Self-deprecating humor was everywhere. Language policing was rare. Words like "tard" or "retard" were colloquialisms by default: "The retard Olympics are going to be awesome next year . . . what was Rio like?" Fist bumps were replaced with nub bumps. Zac's cerebral palsy hand curled in, so I would do the same and we'd bump wrists three times as a secret "handshake". Blind guys, for their goofy fluttering eyes, were dubbed "blinkies." To get a group of blinkies around, they'd often form lines with hands on the shoulders or elbows of the blinky in front of them, blinkiest at the back. Obviously, the professional term for this is a blinky train. You haven't lived until you've seen the undulating caterpillar of an eight-man blinky train navigate the stairs or maneuver a turn. We kept waiting for food trays to fly, expecting blinky crashes, but, amazingly, few ever did. People worked together, and everything went smoothly. I saw more food-tray yard sales in my first day at college than I did over two weeks in an entire village of literal disabled people. So, which group is full of retards again? (*How dare you*). One of the running jokes in Lima became what would happen when I'd meet someone new. I started introducing myself without explaining my category. After a few minutes I'd mention that I was David's guide, which would always be met with levitated eyebrows, popping eyeballs, and a giant "OOOOOOhhhhh." David and I would always laugh, because it had happened yet again: seeing my working limbs and eyes, someone mistook me and my funky mannerisms for a damn T20 instead of a guide. Come to think of it, I probably say words like "resolution" and "abstract structure" too much . . . I may actually have a bit of the bergs.[42]

Jake takes the cake, though, when he ribs Justin with his go-to in dark humor. Years back, Justin was at McDonald's trying to get a viral video going. Justin's buddy was screaming at whoever was behind the counter, "*I SAID NO PICKLES!*" before chucking the sandwich, prompting the discrete, grainy, booth-side screen to bobble around with muzzled laughter. The juvenile pair walked out into the parking lot, bursting at the seams with the boorish chuckling of two dudes in high school making mistakes, still trying to figure it all out. An onlooker followed them outside. As a vet (the military kind), he didn't appreciate these hoodlum's lack of respect. Tempers flared under the

---

[42]   T20 is the mental category of para-athletics who have no physical deformities. This includes people with autism or Asperger syndrome—disabilities that are apparently somewhat local to this author.

soft summer sun amidst the fumes of salty vegetable oil, indifferent to the cortisol crashing through the veins of three frantic deer headbutting in a squalid parking lot. Justin got shot. He ended up with two bullets in his chest, a fragment from one of them finding his spine. Suffice it to say, I needed some backstory while sitting on that bench in Lima. I nearly spit out my food when Jake looked up from his phone, suddenly poking Justin out of the blue, "Bro . . . bro . . . your dick doesn't work because of *pickles*. Fucking *pickles!*" Justin started laughing, shaking his head. "And I *still* pull more women than your bitch ass." Jake rolled his eyes, probably thinking about his girlfriend back home.

The berg's side of my brain squirms with the invalid logic (the pickles weren't causal), but my mostly non-Asperger mind knows that that's beside the point: dark humor builds strength and relieves pressure simultaneously. Despite its function, there's no shortage of people who would flinch at Jake's cutting statement. Women, as well as men with soft hands, have a hard time understanding that sometimes it's necessary to displace compassion for something else. Feminine thinking mistakes the brute stiffness of dark humor as a weapon of aggression rather than as a tool for survival. Like drilling a hole to relieve pressure for a brain that's about to explode, sometimes barbaric means are necessary to avoid barbaric ends. It's not some mystical coincidence that men who slog through tough working conditions, military types and para-athletes, all just happen to naturally be drawn toward gritty, dark humor. If you've ever spent time with these gruff men when they're feeling loose-lipped, you know what I'm talking about. Making light of serious, intense subject matter, like suffering, death, or, even worse, impotence, is a tool which defangs the attack dog. It's a coping mechanism that thickens the skin. If you can be callused enough to embrace a joke about something viscerally negative, then it won't hurt you. If you're tough enough to wrestle with wolves, they won't kill you because they realize you're dangerous enough to fight back. You learn how to have genuine fun in Hell so the impossible-to-ignore, biting truth of your surroundings doesn't rip you to shreds.

Not all comedy is dark of course, but the basic function of all comedy is the same. The value of comedy engages with the truth through levity to replace negative emotion with positive emotion. Even if it's something as simple as a little lighthearted quip to replace an awkward silence with a giggle, comedy still makes the same trade: bad for good through the medium of a laugh. As a professional comedian, Owen Benjamin's entire world operates around this algorithm: truth, levity, and flipping emotion from down to up. It's how he keeps his lights on. You could analyze any of his jokes—especially on his specials—and at the abstract level it's the same thing every time: addressing uncomfortable truths in a way that's funny. Comedians have always had this societal role. It's their job to be the jesters at the king's court. They're beneath contempt, so they jingle away, letting everyone laugh at a few criticisms of their leader(s), critiques that everyone is thinking but no one is saying. Comedians are big, loud, wild, and crass. They push, poke, smile, and laugh. They fight, sneer, shout, and curse. They blurt, yell, squeal, and smirk. Comedians operate on the edge of culture, in the place where discomfort lives undefined. They push boundaries, relieving pressure. If a comedian is doing his job well, he's brash and outspoken, always on the hunt for the next sacred cow. Above all, real comedians refuse to censor themselves.

What does it say, then, about a society that censors comedians? It's analogous to a tyrannical king who chops the head off his jester. In the event of such a partitioning, what you're left with is bloody proof that the jingly-hatted man was right to pester the king. Either the crown was doing something crooked that they really didn't want known, or they can't handle a simple joke. Either way, what you've got is a "leader" that must be criticized. What's great about comedy is how this truth-revealing mechanism is both fun and effective. Lately, the large technocratic corporatocracy engine that drives modern society has been digitally executing dissidents for their lack of compliance. The fact that the growing rumblings of honest criticism is being delivered in the vehicle of a joke only makes it all the more effective. Leading the charge of authentic comedy and counterculture thinking, Big Bear has been systematically removed from corporate platforms. He's been digitally executed for his thoughtcrime. Owen has been kicked off YouTube, PayPal, Instagram, Facebook, Twitter, and a litany of others you've never even heard of. And for what, exactly? For the crime of committing comedy. Just words that people laugh at. The craziest part was when Owen got blackballed from comedy clubs—as a comedian! After SJWs slandered his name with "how dare yous" as some kind of bigot-racist-homophobe for dying on the hill of being opposed to trans-children as an effective comedian, no one wanted to touch him. They complied with the flabby accusations that Owen took comedy too far. Comedy clubs bent the knee and submitted to screeching tyrants who were declaring that joking about supposed victim groups was somehow off the table. Like the para-athletes, us reasonable people know better: victimhood is a state of mind. Nobody is a victim if they make that choice. Everyone with a healthy outlook can appreciate a little self-deprecating humor. Jokes about amputees help amputees. Jokes about Black people help Black people. Jokes about Jews help Jews. What matters is the intent. Owen can, and does, joke about any demographic because he genuinely doesn't hate them. His jokes help them. His levity about the funny parts of Black culture or Jewish culture that no one else is willing to publicly address, is a huge relief for the individual human beings whose group is at the butt end of that joke. Just like with the para-athletes, identity politics is grossly patronizing for everyone.[43] The irony is that this narcissistic, masturbatory behavior of people nannying whole groups of human beings is because they see them as second-class citizens. Victims to be babied. No sensible person wants to be in a priest class.

For his commanding dexterity as a professional jester, Owen Benjamin has proven how empowering the value of comedy is. His entertaining livestream has only grown, thriving despite his digital executions on every major platform and lifetime marketing budget of precisely zero dollars. As a listener, Big Bear's livestream is a welcome reprieve from the blithering idiocy and moral bankruptcy of the mainstream drivel. (*How dare you.*) Regardless of his various axings, Owen refuses to be silenced. Unathorized. tv is prospering. I've seen the Big Bear perform at a church in Vancouver as well as a woodshop in Portland. He taped a special in an airplane hangar. The whole thing has been

---

[43]   Identity politics is the branch of thinking that defines people most fundamentally for what group they belong to, rather than who they are as individuals. It says that every black person is a victim and every white person is an oppressor. It says that victims always have the moral high ground, and that it's the job of legislation to elevate victims economically as well. They see puritanical egalitarianism as utopia. Identity politics is the credo of SJWs, and it's cancerous at every cultural resolution: personal, economical, and institutional. SJW culture and honor culture are incompatible. They can't coexist. We're in a culture war.

very punk rock, except without encouraging the sodomy. Owen's resilience has proven that the stage doesn't make the comedian, the voice does. And what does a stubborn comedian have to say these days? What thoughtcrime is Big Bear perpetuating to be worthy of such brash rejections of the mainstream culture? Just basic honorable morality. Telling the truth. Honest discernment. Not bending the knee to ideologues you know to be nefarious.

Conserving moral, honorable values is the new counterculture. Whether the challenge in your life is overcoming a missing limb or righteously fighting in the culture war for values you know to be good, the value of comedy amounts to the same thing: a tool which leverages us toward the light. Something we can all have gratitude for.

> "There's no prosthetic for an amputated spirit." Wow, what a profound statement.
>
> *Episode #300*

> If you're full of self-hatred, you would see self-depreciation as humiliation, but if you don't have self-hatred, you see it as humility.
>
> *Episode #272*

It's just like I told my son: Just because you're sad doesn't mean you don't put on your boots.

Episode #707

I take something intense [and] I make it joyous.

Episode #750

If there isn't a group of people that directly benefits from [a joke], I don't do it. Because it's just mean.

Episode #797

Sometimes I feel like if I just do a better job with my music or my comedy, I can get you through the pain. I can make you feel enough joy and levity and laughter that you can look at that fucking demon that's right in your face that you can't see cause it's too close.

Episode #802, 1:48:12

When you act like prey, they act like predators.

Comics for censorship is like rabbits for wolves. It's an upside down, backwards way of living. That's like a pacifist special-ops guy. SEAL-team pacifism. It's that crazy.

Episode #225

To complete the circuit of a dramatic example of reality, even if you know what has to come beforehand to show it, the individual has to do it to dramatize it. I knew I would be kicked off Twitter and YouTube. I had to dramatize it. I even did a video that said, "YouTube, I've gotten word that they may kick me off—that will be bad for YouTube. When they do that, it will show the hand." It will show everybody that they won't kick off daily wire even though they're promoting war endlessly through lies, but yet they kick me off [for making jokes and being opposed to child abuse]. That will be bad for YouTube, not me. I was aware of it. I was willing to do that.

March 21, 2020

I will not comply to [nonsense] . . . because compliance is death for me: emotionally, spiritually, professionally. You can't be a comedian and censor your words, you have to trust your instincts . . . that's like being a celibate whore. It's not happening for me, and I think there's value in me explaining this stuff.

Episode #234

More comedy quotes:

You get flack when you're over a target.

Nobody is having more fun than us.

I was releasing a little social stress through satire. That's what comedians are supposed to do.

The Strange Death of Comedy [deleted PragerU video]

Watch an American black guy interact with a fresh off the boat Nigerian, who's even blacker than him, and watch the Nigerian call him a nigger. It's pretty funny.

Episode #300

My job is to point out uncomfortable truths about reality.

Episode #726

When you lose your sense of humor . . . a lot of times that means that you're living a lie. I've seen that happen in my life with people, where they don't see funny anymore. They don't see what's funny. It's because that's the price you pay for living a lie.

Episode #300

We get more watchers in the morning, but in the afternoon it seems like I get a little less apocalyptic.

Episode #292

When you're in a crazy upside-down world and you just stay in absolute fact, it's insanely funny.

Episode #290

You have to explain the joke if society loses its ability to laugh

Episode #302

[Being a comedian is] not the shallow existence of the model and actor. It's still an intellectual exercise. You have to be smart and observant. If you're self-absorbed as a comedian, you don't see anything to make fun of. But you understand both worlds. It creates the daywalker.

Episode #733

Comedian in 2020 is an absurd job.

Episode #708

Think about what is the hill to die on. As a comedian, [my] hill to die on is, you can't censor my words based on nonsense.

Episode #780

My job was always to say uncomfortable truths in a comfortable way.

Episode #733

I'm a comedian and I refuse to kneel.

Episode #731

It just felt good watching comedy do what it was originally supposed to do, which was to mock those in power.

Episode #709

Comedy is a thing. You can try to redefine shit all you want. Comedy is intended to make people laugh—hahahaha—and you have to love your audience in order to accomplish that. You have to love them enough to understand them.

Episode #816, 1:10:05

The comedian sees an obviously ridiculous thing that most people don't see and presents it in a pleasurable way.

Episode #809, 2:39:02

The thing that makes people funny a lot of times is seeing things that are so obvious that other people don't see. Like when the doctor was asking my wife if you wanna also get your tubes tied? . . . That would be like If I was going in for a check-up and they asked, "Do you want to get your balls taken away?"

Episode #809, 2:38:50

The whole point of comedy is to reveal truth. People that don't realize that and try to do comedy are just yelling.

All your truth is going to come from a jester, and all your lies are going to come from the news.

Episode #986, March 21

I get to say the truth. I get to say the truth every day because I'm a goddamn clown. I get to say shit. I get to bring you information and give you stuff that no one else can because their role—their title—would make it impossible. You can't idolize me cause I'm a clown. I'm a comedian. I'm a bard. It's impossible to idolize me.

Episode #1026, April 13

I've always loved the job of comedian, because the jester gets to tell the truth.

Episode #705

That's another thing that dispels fear . . . when someone can see a pattern . . .

How funny is that? It's almost like the normal good guys are [now] seen as weirdos by weirdos.

The bond between comedians and lovers of comedy has to be honest and capable of conflict and capable of coming back together.

The whole point of the comedian is making fun of the sacred cow, so when the sacred cow used to be various institutions and they applauded it, it was only because they were pushing toward degeneracy. Now the sacred cow is degeneracy.

Episode #732

This is why a comedian is such a good truth-teller, because I was trained in clubs surrounded by strangers, and if what I said wasn't true on a metaphysical base level . . . they didn't laugh. And that's why I always had the podcast *Why Didn't They Laugh*: because I was searching for the truth.

Episode #795

It's as obvious as the nose on your face

Episode #552

George is deep state.

Life's still funny when you keep your soul.

193

If you love someone, you've got to make sacrifices. So, anyway, back to the nigger thing.

Episode #208

Where's my kazoo? It's okay, I have backup kazoos.

Episode #225

Why is the mustache ridiculed? Because it's a sign of masculinity and it's unapologetic.

The population of Canada is like, ten. Just have eight kids and tell them to fuck off.

My dad teaches rhetoric. He may as well have taught at Hogwarts.

Jeranism show

I take comedy seriously.

CHAPTER 9

Value of Gratitude

We've come a long way now. Imagine the upgrade in mental landscape for a man or woman who has unearthed buried honorable values: speaking honestly, deciphering discernment, embracing discomfort, upholding courage, asserting masculinity, safeguarding freedom, and creating comedy. Absolutely life changing. Like the many ingredients of a nourishing meal, however, the whole thing can become noxious with the mold of bitterness. A cynical, peevish little man can technically qualify as upholding the values put forward in chapters 1 through 8 and still be a wretch. An outspoken bloodhound—despite his discernment and honesty—is alienating. A cranky curmudgeon—despite his courage and masculinity—is repulsive. A sarcastic fink—despite his unrestrained humor—is contemptible. Just think of the top five people who you dislike spending time around. Are they grateful human beings? I doubt it. More likely they're ornery, resentful, and petulant. It simply isn't fun being near someone who is in a pit of despair, skulking around with a chronic sense of bitterness at the outrageous unfairness of what's local or universal, governmental or personal, or physical or metaphysical. The context doesn't change the outcome, because a peevish person will always find something to complain about. Their circumstance isn't the problem. Their mindset is the problem.

My college days were laced with the germinating mold of bitterness. My parents set me out on a good path, but without understanding the environment they had no chance against the steep hill of moral degradation progressively imposed on me by public school, Hollywood, and mainstream culture. Year after year, my mindset deteriorated. In my fourth year at college I became an irritable, self-abusive, indulgent shut-in, locked in my room playing video games with breaks bound to food, running practice, and daily pornos. Class was a write-off. A recovering addict might diagnose this year as "hitting rock bottom." In the years that followed I clambered out of cerebral hell, scrubbing the sickly mold off my mind one long, slow, day at a time. There's no shortage of people who are still in the cavernous depths that I once occupied. I'd like to help explain what's going on and shine some light on the circumstance. We can just ignore the horde of undiscerning voices that would indignantly caterwaul against my perspective on mental health. They can spatter forth accusations of ignorance, apathy, or even cruelty all they like. I don't care. Their hair-triggered "how dare yous" are set off at the slightest hint of individual responsibility. However, depression isn't a prison sentence. It's self-imposed. (*How dare you.*) Although I don't lend credence to the loudest voice in the room simply for its amplitude, I will rein myself in a tad on this this touchy issue for its broadness. I'll speak for myself only.

There was nothing wrong with me. I mean, okay, constant crippling negative emotion? Check. Hopelessly unable to do anything productive? Check. Clinically diagnosed for a "mental health issue"? Check. But I stand by my (amended) statement: there was nothing *inherently* wrong with me. My instincts were telling me that there was a problem, *and there was*. My mind wasn't mistaken about reality. The toaster wasn't talking to me—I wasn't mentally ill. The feeling of anxiety was a correct response for the situation: I shouldn't have been in school. My feeling of depression was accurate for the reality of my circumstance: I was wrong to be a morally bankrupt degenerate on a deadly descending path. Like a body ingesting poison, the painful symptoms of my mind were exactly appropriate. The effect of my problem was mental suffering. But the cause? My own failure to have a morally upright compass. My own failure to build the basic framework conducive to refusing despair. My own failure to seek honorable values.

Looking back, what should my perspective now be about this whole ordeal? How should I internalize my quasi-intentional seven—yes, *seven*—infantilizing years spent at school just to get an undergraduate degree in a field I will never work in? How should I feel about going into mid-five-figures of student debt in exchange for an experience that savagely ravaged my mind, spiraling me down into guilt, depression, and despair? How should I feel about such a monumental failure to spend my foremost years on something even remotely positive? Simple: I should feel gratitude.

I'm grateful for my cataclysmic disaster of a school experience for the simple reason that it's by far the best option available. Call me a pragmatist. Being a disgruntled little sourpuss provides precisely nothing helpful. I can bitch and moan and wallow in self-pity about how hard it was for me, or I can think about all the immensely productive lessons and values learned explicitly through deep discomfort. Which sounds like the better approach? Gratitude or despair? Either feeling can be justified based on something true, or even discerned, because both gratitude and despair are self-appointed perspectives. Life can be beautiful or life can be shit, it just depends on whether you choose to look at it through the eyes or the asshole.

What I choose to focus the spotlight of my mind on is what sets the stage. My attention can be directed at despair or captivated by gratitude; they're both available to me, ready and waiting. This book never would have been written if I hadn't made the deliberate decision to embrace gratitude and reflect, positively, about what I learned through hard lessons. When you see human beings radiating with fulfillment, it's important to know that they made that choice. It's left to you to either envy or admire their decision, because you're entirely capable of either. Your perspective can be bitter or grateful. Your charge can be negative or positive. Your ethos can be despair or gratitude. The context doesn't change the nature of your free will once you recognize how it works; you can always choose to move up the hill regardless of how steep it is. Sheer cliff? Time to get out the carabiners.

There's no shortage of people who struggle to find gratitude in the face of immense discomfort. It's a tall albeit completely possible order—I highly recommend it. For every successful para-athlete who climbed her way out of Hell with a smile on her face there's a dozen who didn't, sitting angry and bitter on the couch, collecting government checks, watching pixels dance, shitting in bags, alone. One of the things I noticed about para-athletes is that some were only partway out of the pit of despair, still figuring it out. For them, the value of comedy—especially dark comedy—was the only tool in their toolkit. They couldn't take anything seriously for its vulnerability. For the people capable of dark comedy, anything *could* be a joke, but for those dependent on it, everything *was* a joke. These guys were coping, not thriving. To take the next step required diversifying their toolkit, becoming adept with more than just the shield of comedy, becoming adept with the vision of gratitude.

Having gratitude is a skill like breathing is a skill: everyone can do it, some are better at it than others, and doing so is necessary to thrive. Some people think that the phrase "breathing is a skill" sounds like something a crazy person would say, but it's true! Once again, I'll use myself as an example. Since I naturally have a big heart and lungs, and I've spent my whole life rigorously exercising, the modus operandi of my entire breathing apparatus is, in a word, excellent.[44] While under the coaching staff of one of Canada's national training centers, I was required to record my heart rate several times daily. Every morning I'd strap on a monitor, take a few deep breaths, and watch the arithmetic pixels plunge: 37 bpm, 34 bpm, 31 bpm, NO READ. The damn thing couldn't read below 30 beats per minute, so most mornings I'd be forced to guess. The majority of my logbook entries would read: "Morning heart rate: 28?" As a consequence of having a resting heart

---

[44]   Intense exercise will literally make a heart grow in size, just like any other muscle.

rate low enough to make most doctors wonder if their machine is broken, it's literally easier for me to breathe. Try limiting your breathing to two long slow breaths per minute like I can comfortably do. Thirteen seconds in, seventeen seconds out. Then do it again. And again. And again. Gasping for air yet?

Like air to the lungs, how easily your subconscious positive emotion flows depends upon your mental fitness. So, how mentally fit are you? How honest? How discerning? How free? Mental fitness comes from mental exercise. Do you actively speak the truth? Do you practice the discomfort of discernment and seriously investigate perspectives you disagree with? Do you exercise an appreciation of goodness every day? It's a feedback loop. On the kinetic side, the most physically talented men and women enjoy exercise the most, so they seek it out with the greatest intensity and frequency. Consequently, they get a double benefit: the raw talent and the hard work. In contrast, those without physical gifts shy away from exercise, getting the double whammy in the opposite direction: lack of talent and a lack of hard work. This combination of orientation and projection creates a great divide: Elite athletes and couch potatoes are like different species. Yesterday, I sold a planter box to a pleasant man wearing a caroonkoo mask. He seemed embarrassed as he explained through heavy breathing how he was only wearing the mask because he was at high risk of catching the virus and he promised his wife he'd don the garb.

His oxygen deficit, however, was a consequence of both the purple veil covering his mucus-inclined face-holes *and* his poor health. His swollen ankles, sagging belly, and creaky gait betrayed a pre-sixty-year expiration date. Five minutes after he arrived, I was glad to see him shed some of his insecurity. He removed the purple veil off his face and started making jokes with me. Despite enjoying our wisecracks, I couldn't completely detach from an uncomfortable awareness of his gasping for breath. His body was fighting for air because his health was in jeopardy. Standing a few feet apart, we were the personification of two ends of the health spectrum. My extreme includes running fast and breathing well. His extreme includes struggling to stand on the ground. And an early death.

While I have an affinity for physicality, I'm certainly no savant when it comes to gratitude. I can relate to the awkwardness of trying to work on something you're not naturally gifted at. Regardless, poor fitness in any domain is a losing proposition. In the throes of college, my mind was as unfit and unhealthy as that man's body. Like him, just managing basic tasks was a struggle. To a grateful person, both gifted and well practiced in the mental exercise of pursuing gratitude, my despair would seem ludicrous, like struggling to stand on the ground. We'd be like different species: one floating on the water, happily buoyant on the balmy fluid, the other desperately thrashing about in a mad sputtering panic, two absurdly different modes in this same medium we call the human experience. Luckily for me, practicing gratitude is something anyone can do. It just takes some effort.

Inevitably, part of successfully navigating life is seeing its inherent duality. Every vice has a virtue. Every gap has a gift. Every loss has a lesson. It reminds me of Robert Stevenson's famous work, *Dr. Jekyll & Mr. Hyde*. In Stevenson's tale, Dr. Jekyll is an admired doctor who concocts a potion. Upon drinking said crazy-sauce, he transforms into the brutish Mr. Hyde. Y'know, just like how Hollywood, media, and college affects young people: transforming them from respectable, capable, and upstanding human beings into garish, squawking, disastrous troglodytes. Upon reflection, Dr. Jekyll realizes the primitive dual nature of man. Among other thinkers, Carl Jung expanded on this duality-of-man concept in his writings where he details the "persona" and the "shadow." Jung claimed that as people develop, two systems form simultaneously: the persona (like Dr. Jekyll), and the shadow (like Mr. Hyde), the former being the socially acceptable side of human nature, with the latter being closer to a humanities major. As a fractal component of people, individual emotions also exhibit a kind of shadow duality. Fortunately, this is a two-way street. While every virtue has its vice, every vice also has its virtue. With enough mental fitness, even the seven deadly sins can be reoriented into something gracious. Greed can be reoriented to ambition. Sloth can be reoriented to rest. Envy can be re-oriented to admiration. Pride can be reoriented to dignity. Wrath can be reoriented to righteousness. Gluttony can be reoriented to nourishment. And lust can be reoriented to passion. A subtle tweak, and the whole world changes.

What each of these dualities pervading the human experience has in common is the underlying opportunity for free choice. No matter the circumstance, the human being within it has the ability to choose their response. Grappling with gratitude is not about circumstance, it's about perspective. However, the purpose of gratitude isn't to justify a failure for change. If your situation sucks, change it! Gratitude is, in a technical sense, a path-dependent property: the order in which you do things matters. The value of gratitude isn't chapter 1 of this book for a reason; you shouldn't feel positively about dishonesty. A lack of basic moral values is a legitimate reason to feel negative emotion. During my college degeneracy, while still lazily floating downwards it would have been inappropriate for me to try to force myself to feel positively about my circumstance. Only after realizing which direction is up and making a conscious push for it was it reasonable to feel grateful for the hard lessons my suffering taught me. The appropriateness of gratitude depends upon the context of the path you choose to apply it to. Gratitude isn't an excuse to feel great about moral degradation, its purpose is to positively engage with whatever challenge happens to present itself as you move forward, aiming up. That's important: Gratitude is only appropriate *if you're aiming up.* It's a very different thing than trying to trick yourself into feeling grateful for your lazy descent. Get the basics right, then smile at whatever comes next, no matter how challenging.

Fortunately for us, nothing is ever going to be perfect. Our glitches are good, because limitation is interwoven into the genesis of life's meaning. We live as blessedly flawed beings, primitive meat suits for a divine spark bumbling about in a chaotic ether. Every scenario that includes a human being is by definition imperfect. This leaves much to be open to interpretation. What inspires gratitude in you inspires despair in someone else. A dozen chickens? So much work! School was hell for me, but I refuse to look back on it through the lens of bitterness. I'm grateful for the opportunity to reflect and act upon what I've learned through my catastrophes. A loss truly is a lesson. Or at least it can be. With the right fundamental values, gratitude can be found just as easily in the test of scarcity as it can in the bounty of abundance. Every injustice is a test of character. Our viper pit of politics is an opportunity to reject rage. Our fool's gold of Hollywood is an opportunity to reject envy. Our culture of consumption is an opportunity to reject gluttony. Our propaganda of pixels is an opportunity to reject sloth. Our cerebral cake of porn is an opportunity to reject lust. Our promotions of family-shattering proportions are an opportunity to reject greed. Our fancy-pants status symbols are an opportunity to reject pride. If you care to really look, you'll see that the predatory aspect of our technocratic corporatocracy culture is appalling, but that's no excuse to abandon starting a family in a fit of pathetic despair; finding moral integrity in the face of horror is a test of your strength of character. The value of gratitude orients the totality of honorable values in their proper, fulfilling direction, but to choose such a challenging path you must exercise embracing it.

> You're going to spend your life fighting in a matrix you created with your own despair.

Episode #611

> I'm not able to be depressed. I can't allow myself that indulgence.

> No one has done any of these nightmares that you think they're going to do. You've done it to yourself, every day with stress, depression, despondency, not being close to your family, your friends, watching pornography, eating bad, drinking, being on pharmaceutical drugs.

Episode #677

That's how you float, that's how you rise, that's how you be in the world but not of it . . . when you're even grateful for the wicked.

Episode #804, 1:41:08

Do you know what victim consciousness does to you? It makes it so you never feel gratitude.

Episode #705

For all the nice weather in the world, you have to have rain or else [nothing] grows. When you see a lush green beautiful day, all the green comes from water that comes from the sky that everyone [complains] about.

Episode #292

I'm doing this to free the people who keep coming to me with their bullshit despair, telling me what to be scared of . . . you have to go or change . . . you can't bring despair here. It's a sickness.

Episode #802, 1:44:39

The best vector for murder is your own hand.

March 22, 2020

Despair is only when you think short term . . . just stay the path.

Episode #728

Everybody has their Achilles. Y'know, if you're brave and courageous, your Achilles will be being too impulsive because you're like, "My gut says this, we do it," without fear. If you're patient and cautious, your Achilles heel will be stagnation . . . it's a wave, guys, it's always a wave. Envy and admiration is the same wave it's just that envy is the subversion of admiration. To look up to somebody as a role model is very good, to look up to in envy is very bad. It's the same with courage and impulsiveness, patience and stagnation, love and lust . . . it's the upside down versus the right side up of every wave.

Episode 833, 33:49

You should have shame. Just because you say "unashamed" doesn't mean you shouldn't have any shame.

March 22, 2020 stream

Despair will keep you from having a family and it'll make you sick. So, it's not really an option to just put your head in the sand, but at the same time you can't do anything about it, so just enjoy yourself. Have a good life.

Episode #709

More gratitude quotes:

The opposite of despair is gratitude.

Look at the sun through the leaves, and have gratitude.

The thing they're always trying to take from you is gratitude.

Episode #653

Being a victim is a choice.

I quit drinking because I realized the world isn't going to end.

Episode #532

I ban despair.

Despair is cancer. There is nothing good from despair. When you feel despair say, "That is cancer," and cut it out.

Episode #483

There is no despair here. If you come near it, you are banned.

I've been demonetized but not demoralized.

Episode #695

I like being around these giant trees because it's the one time in my life I feel small and safe.

IG stream

All right, here's some advice for ya: Try to go a day without starting a sentence with the word "I". Try to go a day without once saying "me," "I," or "my," and just see what it does to your mind.

Episode #708

Hate is cheap.

Episode #787

Watch out for people pushing despair, they are all wrong.

If you're always disappointed in someone, you're abusing them.

People will sometimes just re-adapt to despair.

Episode #810

Dreaming of good stuff, of what you could be. Gratitude of what you enjoy. These are prayers, whether you say amen or not.

Episode #711

And by the way, having something to live for is a lot more powerful than something that you would die for.

I have a healthy distrust of my own mind.

The least you can do is not have so much despair.

Episode #679

CHAPTER 10

Value of Family

At this point in the book we've made some decent progress culling the herd. Nothing like extricating a few "how dare yous" from the undesirables to keep it lean. However, we've only rocked the boat, we've yet to flip it. The SJWs were a write-off well before we closed chapter 6. Most people, however, are reasonable enough to consider "bigoted" ideas as outrageous as "men aren't toxic" without having their heads explode. Good thing, too. But now it's time to ruffle even the moderates' feathers. You can sink, fly, or swim, but no more free rides. Time to get to risky business—enough of the cautious stuff. Now we're turning the dial up to eleven. Now we're cooking with gas. Now we're riding this gravy train of honor culture right into the heart of our society's secular engine to see how the fucker ticks. We're going to replace a few rusty cogs clogging our failed civil machine, supplanting the puritanical egalitarianism of feminism with a strong family unit. In other words, we're going to address something controversial: women shouldn't work. (*How dare you!*)

First things first. If your heart is racing, relax. It's just words. Ink on a page. Pixels on a screen. A thought in the ether. Exploring ideas you don't believe in is part of the discernment process. Know, dear feather-ruffled reader, that I'm trying to do my best by exploring ideas and getting to the discerned truth about how best to operate as a culture. If you're still upset after knowing that my intent is honest, genuine, and altruistic, then it's now a *you* issue. You're responsible for your rage; I'm not inflicting anything on you. The ability to consider opinions controversial to your own without bleeding from your ears is the test of a healthy mind. Practice the discomfort of healthy thinking.

Part of any strong culture is the role of strong families. In the tyrannical nightmare of *1984*, it's no surprise that Big Brother broke families, dismantling them into dysfunction with the fear of a Hulk smash. In *Brave New World*, the world controllers snapped the same ties but they managed it with the bribe of indulgence, both sides of the tyrannical coin buying the same thing: atomization. When it comes to the strategies of a tyrant, preventing large gatherings of people is communism 101. Crushing the family unit is the master class. Fortunately, selling out to the freshly minted greed of debt or the iron-shackled fear of pain is far from an inevitability. Wise men and women understand that all currencies are not created equal.

Void of honor, mainstream culture has become scared for its failure to be self-reliant and fat for its failure to delay gratification. Whether you believe contemporary culture has been crafted with tyrannical, malicious intent or simply formed as a reaction to the will of people in a democratic marketplace is up for debate. Either way, the outcome simply is what it is: modern secular society has become atomized. It's become soft. Moldable. Pliable. Isolated individuals, bound by weak bonds, are much easier to control. A weak man, hooked on drugs, pornos, and video games, isn't capable of saying no to a tyrannical leader or a degenerating algorithm, while a strong man with his own source of food, a discerning mind, and a loving family, is. The latter actualizes a great life that's admirable, honorable, and fulfilling. The former dismantles society.

Feminism, as a derivative of our culture's egalitarian core, has become integral to the mainstream narrative. The beating heart of our modern civil culture bleeds for equality between all people. Overstuffed men and women pat themselves on their puffy backs for such "virtuous" positions without even knowing what feminism means, what it does, or how it would be enforced. Equality of what? Money? Be specific. How is it implemented? Is it just? What's the effect? Due diligence aside, feminists, bound by their holy commandment of egalitarianism, have pushed for "equity." Now these doctrines have become dogma: *Thou shalt not have a joint bank account.* Feminism is treated with reverence, while intellectually honest appeals to honorable family values are decried as heresy. You want to marry and be the sole provider for a housewife and kids? How dare you. Typical sexist bigot. Forgive this sexist bigot, but I can't help it: my greatest goal in life is to forge a strong, healthy, loving family. Such hope is in fundamental opposition to feminism.

Standing right-side up, it's clear that our upside-down culture has "elevated" women to their descent. Women are convinced that being used and abandoned for a fresher model like a truck-stop whore (*how dare you*) while they scramble to get out from under the weight of their debt for a useless degree is somehow ideal. Let me spell it out: Casual sex and debt slavery isn't empowerment. We've all been tricked. Somewhere along the line, the cultural narrative shifted. Instead of encouraging men to do better, now women are encouraged to do worse. Instead of elevating, mainstream culture descends. Instead of taking personal risks to help others (like an honorable knight), modern men and women make personal gains by risking others (like a civilized banker). As a consequence, the mainstream cultural ethic is morally bankrupt. Forget integrity, logical consistency, or avoiding hypocrisy, just do as though wilt: have no shame for shameful actions, ignore consequences for what's consequential, and pretend there's no reason to be reasonable. Mainstream civil culture is just collective whimsical promotion of chronic selfish indulgence. It's an insult to our nature.

The cultural experiment has run its course. The conclusion is definitive: atomization is a disaster. Feminism is a catastrophe. It's a cancer. It's a wart. It's an untreated malignant tumor jeopardizing the health of the system. Unfortunately, women who buy in don't find out until they're childless and alone on a couch at forty, crying into a vegan-cheese sandwich wondering why a giant bank account, several dudes named Chad, and a few Chad-related abortions made them feel so empty.

In the pursuit of discerning the value of family, there's an inevitable need to better understand egalitarianism and how it prompted feminism. However, it's a tad dry. Like the parchedness of TNT, the whole package is set to explode into a cataclysm of finicky subsections, philosophical jargon, and political angles, a blast radius just begging for distracted readers. In addition to its volatility, such an analysis is also complicated enough to be a bit above my pay grade. For its web of intricacy, we're bound to get stuck in the trap of traditional dialectic analysis. Instead of dishing up a sticky word salad with a side of crunchy bugs, I'm just going to tell a story. Nobody likes eating bugs.[45]

After my "rock bottom" year in college, I was on a new path: getting out of the hole I was in and building up a different life. The reconstruction was my own choice that started with packing my bags: new school, new coach, new friends. After I moved, I was lucky enough to find myself in a scrappy college house with a bunch of great dudes. Within this group of guys, my social role manifested itself as a kind of jokester character. My quirks, scatterbrain thinking, and absurd life circumstances combined to express themselves as a great big gaff. Part of the goofiness was inextricably tied to how out of sorts I was internally. Rather than be crushed by reality, comedy served me well as a brace, misdirecting the weight of the world. Years later, my sense of enthusiastic humor has only grown, although the nature of it has changed. I love to joke around, and do it all the time, but I'm no longer dependent on the crutch of comedy. Now, underneath everything, the satire is for its own sake. I don't need to misdirect anymore. I scrapped the clown makeup, happy to look reality in the face without any misdirection. My genuine values scrubbed away the need for anything synthetic. I actively make the attempt to showcase what's inside, hiding nothing,

---

[45]   Hey Internet! Quit trying to make everyone eat bugs! It's gross!

because authenticity is king. It's the immorality of a man that begs for the shelter of a mask.

Every other weekend or so, I still get together with these guys. They're first-rate buddies, the kind of guys you always enjoy seeing. Interestingly, we still default to our old imprinted roles. With this group of dudes, I'm still assigned the role of class clown despite its mismatch to my life now. The map is imprinted into an old landscape, set when we first bonded in the house we shared. Now when they ask about my circumstance, underneath their questions is often the hope for a farcical comic gem. They're mining for absurdity in an old vacant quarry. This creates an odd incongruity between their expectations driven by my irresponsible past and reality driven by my conscientious present. Although I like to joke, the direct answers to their questions often involve something astute, like the value of honesty, faith, or family. Trying to see such austere concepts through the lens of parody turns out to be a kind of gaff of its own.

A few months ago, my friends and I got together for a board-game night. The guy hosting shares an apartment that his girlfriend bought on a loan. As a couple they're a good match. They're both genuine, good-hearted people. The mainstream culture would present them as the textbook ideal for modern millennials. Late twenties, no kids, not even close (but probably one or two down the line). They're both smart, they went to college, and work independently. They studied geography, history, and the labyrinth of legislation. Each of them is a posterchild for the affable moderate. They're kind people who lean left, committed to trusting the mainstream narratives: guns are bad, abortion is good, and democracy is king. [46] Preferring to avoid the hard conversations, they're exemplars of sociable decorum: constantly thinking about how their actions affect others, careful to ensure everyone gets along. Raising a fuss at thanksgiving, a restaurant, or in a supermarket is unthinkable. They never shout or draw attention to themselves in public—ever. Their actions are measured. In a conversation they're careful not to offend, always offering a hesitant preamble for anything mildly controversial; they leave any real cause for altercation in the untouched shadowy corners of the naughty box. They're extremely civilized.

After the pieces found their box and the box found its shelf, we found ourselves in the typical hour of closing conversation. Though we had shifted from the game of Catan to the game of life, the topics of discussion, curiously enough, stayed the same: plans to specialize, settlement ambitions, and resource acquisition. We talked about career goals. We talked about where we wanted to live. We talked about money. One of the topics outside of the triad of typical conversation was religion. I had

---

[46]   The irony is intentional. I'm looking forward to writing my next book about politics.

expressed my contentedness with my recent pursuit of Christianity.

"Really? Christianity? Don't you think it's hypocritical? I mean, the whole do-anything-bad-and-just-confess-it-away thing?" He started grinning, expecting something absurd in my response.

"No, dude. The purpose of confession is just to acknowledge intent."

"Oh," he responded, his eyes suddenly filling with the flash of purpose.

When I saw his response, it was like I could hear the satisfying sound of a puzzle piece clicking into place in his mind. Something he could already see came into focus, resolving itself: The purpose of confession is to authentically acknowledge our flaws and try to do better. It's not supposed to be a get-out-of-jail-free card that helps us sin more. It's a conscious acknowledgement of the poor behavior that puts us there in the first place! True repentance recognizes the importance of intent by addressing it honestly, then frees the person from their misdeeds so they can try to do better next time. It solves the problem of lying to yourself and pretending that sin is good to avoid the pain of moral failure. It also solves the problem of being weighted down by the truth of sinful behavior. There's a difference between consciously aiming for sin and unintentionally falling short of an honorable decision to refuse it. Intent matters.

Getting to share knowledge that lands is rewarding for bravos like me.[47] I love helping others do better. Later that same evening, however, I was unable to elicit the same quality of answer to a different question, this time put forward by his girlfriend.

"So, you want a housewife to cook and clean for you?" she quipped incredulously.

"I mean . . . yeah," I slowly responded, uncertain but eventually committing.

This question stuck with me for months. It sticks with me now. I wouldn't be surprised if it sticks with me for life, but not because I missed some of the obvious maid jokes. I didn't feel right about my response, which was odd, because I do want to marry a woman who commits to the role of a housewife. Eventually, I discerned the source of my internal dissonance. My answer was wrong. I got tripped up by the orientation of the question. The trap that caught me was tacked on the end: "Do you want a housewife to cook and clean *for you*?" It's the "for you" that makes the genuinely correct answer to that specific binary a definitive no. I do imagine marrying a loving housewife. I do imagine being the sole provider of resources. I do

---

[47]   Check out the "Socio-Sexual Hierarchy" by Voxiversity: voxday.blogspot.com. "Beta" has since been renamed "Bravo" to avoid the hook-up culture connotation, which defines a Beta as ubiquitous to "undesirable man."

imagine her being in charge of taking care of our home—
but not for me, for the whole family.

Therein lies the profound flaw of feminism: it's
selfish. Feminism claims to champion empowered, strong,
independent women. But the way they promote their
supposed wonder-women is through the bank account.
They inspire women to choose money, psychiatrists,
and a hefty dose of antidepressants to cope with their
abandonment of family. Punching nonsense data into
nonsense algorithms for a nonsense company is a far cry
from seeing the light of God in the eyes of your child. But
they do it anyway for status and shiny things. Feminists
would have women believing that their nature is somehow
the problem. That wanting to care for a baby is a symptom
of a woman's oppression. That women are victims. That
the feeling of emptiness and despair is a consequence of
some nebulous problem like mental health, sexism, or the
patriarchy, rather than the murderously poisonous lifestyle
that feminism promotes. It's an irresponsible philosophy
at best, and a noxiously malicious one at worst. The entire
metric wielded by feminists to measure a woman's success
compares individual women's cash flows to individual
men's cash flows. Like Huxley's world controllers or
Orwell's Big Brother, feminists atomize their perspective
right down to the individual, completely shattering any
hope of focusing on the whole family. Their narcissistic
resolution doesn't allow for it. They're too zoomed in.
They're too stubborn, antagonistic, and selfish to take the

necessary step back to see the bigger picture of caring for a family. Feminists do the nasty work of either tyrants or a heartless degenerating algorithm (or both); they shatter strong families, creating miserable, lonely, shrieking harpies in the process.[48]

"Look to your leaders," feminists say. "Be like Ellen." "Be like Oprah." "Be like Beyoncé." In other words, be a childless, grotesque, morally bankrupt baron, obsessed with equal parts money, status, and power.[49] Of course, these extremes aren't what normal, non-demonic people will achieve. If you're one of the 99.999 percent, then the question isn't whether you'll get to the end of the road, but rather, which road are you traveling down? Which direction are you headed? What's your orientation? Are you consciously aiming at prioritizing for your family? If that's the case, women should aspire to be in charge of the tasks at home for a family that loves them, instead of working as a debt slave for an institution that hates them. Leave the corporate salt mines to the man. He's better at dealing with such insanity anyway. A good man can provide resources for the woman to take care of the whole

---

[48] Also, a legion of well-intentioned moderates who, thinking they're doing the right thing, abandon the idea of kids in their twenties and frantically pop out a single lonely child at thirty-four. But that doesn't make for the best rhetoric, so shrieking harpies it is.

[49] Try doing some serious research into the lives of these women when they're off camera. They're insidious human beings.

family.[50] It's his job. That's God's moral law; the roles that we're adapted to; the tasks that we're built for. Will you truly abandon your children for more money?

Women today are told that the most virtuous behavior they can express is that of a degenerate man: indulgence, debt slavery, and casual sex. They're told by feminists that femininity itself is a transgression. Men feel very differently. Strong men don't care if you're a business tycoon at all. Not one bit. We care about the traits of a good wife: health, fertility, and compassion.[51] In contrast, feminists indignantly advocate that blowing up into sarcastic blubbery land whales, for example, is virtuous, while taking care of yourself is a sin. An altruistic (albeit naive) person, projecting good intent onto others, will respond, "Why is feminism condemning femininity?

---

[50]   If every woman didn't work, the supply of labor would half, doubling its value. Although free mobility of labor, technology, and usury are breaking the supply/demand mold, hypothetically (in classical economics) a single man could make the same real earnings as a man and a woman. At the resolution of the family, the same amount of money would be coming in, except in this version of things, the children aren't abandoned to the hell of daycare. Even if the total money coming in goes down, trading some money for a stronger, more content family is well worth it for the honorable parent.

[51]   Physical beauty, by the way, is just a derivative of fertility. Symmetry suggests good genetics, which means healthy babies. A curvy 0.7 waist-to-hip ratio also suggests fertility.

I'm so confused! Why is degeneracy considered angelic while health and beauty are demonized?" The answer is simple: they're candy people. The feminist doctrine is perfectly logical . . . based on its assumptions. It faithfully follows its preeminent dictum of financial equity based on peevish envy and malicious hatred of men. Feminism isn't some well-intentioned philosophy that unknowingly hurts women. Feminists are the kamikaze pilots of culture. Feminists deliberately strike out against men, happy to hurt women in the process. It's just the cost of doing business. Feminism sacrifices women on the altar of progressivism in a wanton explosion of Cheeto dust, insane debt, and twerking for a political angle that's about as feminine as a pump-action shotgun. Just pump and shoot, pump and shoot, pump and shoot. Casual sex with a drunk puffer fish? No thanks. (*How dare you.*)

Ironically, by trying so hard to push against the men they hate, feminists have become defined by those same men. They don't do what's best for women at all. They just do whatever's the worst for men. The fungus of feminism has culturally mushroomed into a poisonous wretch of a plant.[52] Algorithms are a hell of a thing. Feminism has, by its inevitable egalitarian conclusion, made every attempt to eliminate the very differences between men and women that make the bonding experience so gratifying. Instead

---

[52] Technically, fungi are no longer considered plants. They're placed in a separate kingdom. Oh well.

of puzzle pieces that fit together, feminists are pushing for perfectly mirrored, completely isolated squares unable to connect for their symmetry. Feminist nagging applauds feminine men and masculine women. They cheer for a sexually amorphic culture, one big, gross, gray stew. In its delusional scramble to manufacture vapid Ken dolls, the feminist doctrine has become so treacherously upside down that it genuinely views Hell as Heaven. Their ethics are evil. The newly nurtured baby of feminism is literally the most extreme form of reprobate hypocrisy that's ever existed: abortion.

How dare you? Yeah, we know. And we get it, feminists get mad when normal people try to save babies. But the thing is, that doesn't matter. How some blue-hair gender-studies major feels about something doesn't change the truth of it. Abortion is the archetype, or fundamental representation, of hypocrisy. Nothing in the world is more hypocritical than abortion. My claim for this is a technical one. It is built upon the simple definition of hypocrisy: rules for thee, not for me. It's a basic violation of the principle of fairness. Why is abortion the most extreme violation of rules for thee, not for me? Well . . . because it is. The hypocrisy found in abortion is built right into the misleadingly soft language of its mainstream title: *pro-choice.* They're advocating for autonomy—the ability to freely choose. These pro-abortion advocates push their mantra to the extreme; they argue that a woman should be legally permitted to make the most excessively immoral decision possible: terminating (or killing) a baby. It should go without saying by the way, that a choice doesn't get more extreme than killing a baby . . . it's killing a baby. How this affects hypocrisy is simple. Besides the harrowing sense of guilt and loss, the implications of killing a baby are, of course, the removal of that baby's ability to make his or her own choices. A dead baby can't choose anything. You removed her choices when you killed her. Pro-abortion advocates are saying, "My choices include removing others' choices." How many of those choices? All of them. And against whom? The most innocent in the world. It's the most extreme freedom to choose for the would-be mother with the most extreme removal of free choice simultaneously from the baby. Rules for thee, not for me, pushed as far apart as it could possibly go. Not one thing in the world is more hypocritical than abortion, to say nothing of the evil of *killing a baby*.

All this to say, the failure of feminists to repent is a *them* issue. Feminists can face the reality of what killing a baby is or not. Either way, the rest of us are just going to keep going. There's no stopping the pursuit of truth. Abortion is hypocrisy; abortion is evil; abortion is legal. Doesn't matter. Moral people don't need the nauseating institution of government to tell them how to behave. They also don't need to be validated by it. I don't care what some bird-brained career politician has to say. I don't need Bernie or any of the Bernie Bros in Portland to tell me what's moral. Even if his hypocritical dogma can afford him plenty of houses, he isn't permitted real estate in my mind. Moral women reject abortion legislation by simply not getting abortions. Moral men provide the environment necessary to make women feel safe enough to do so. Alternatively, the institution of government or any of its representatives have nothing whatsoever to do with ethics, values, or morality in any capacity. Indignant SJWs can get smolderingly righteous about chopping up babies for face cream all they want.[53] I do not consent.

Luckily for honorable, moral people, consciousness is rising. The "how dare you" weapon, like the system of progressive values, is becoming duller by the day. Social shame just doesn't have the same biting edge that it used to. *"How dare you say abortion is hypocritical!"* Swing goes the rubber axe of social shame. *"How dare you say abortion is evil!"* Flop goes the limp, fragile knife of the SJW ego. *"How dare you . . . SIR!"* Doesn't matter. They see themselves as warriors with weapons. Everyone else sees them as toddlers with rattlers. For years, SJWs have been screeching and squawking, tiring themselves out in a manic, decades-long temper tantrum. Once commanding, their juvenile squealing is now falling on deaf ears. Without infants to take care of, feminists have become babies themselves. It's no matter. The forest of

---

[53]   If you don't know what I'm talking about, check out the interview of Sandra Bullock and Ellen talking about baby-dick face cream.

truth will just keep growing. Benevolent human beings are learning that social shame can be a weapon, rendering the one tool in the SJW toolbox ineffective. Ear plugs are cheap. Like countless others, the shame mob doesn't make decisions for me like it used to because I understand what they're doing: manipulating the good intent of altruistic people by screaming at them. The whole strategy has been completely defanged. Being shamed into a worse human being is a fading trend. (*How . . . how dare you?*)

For the "how dare you" people who still don't like the idea that women shouldn't work, you can relax, it's not the 1920s anymore. Everyone is in the same boat on this: honorable men aren't posturing to abolish the equal pay act of 1963; we're all on board egalitarianism when it comes to the most basic legislation. We're trying to create a culture that, in general, encourages free women to be mothers. We're not trying to legally force women into cages to be our breeding sows. At the grown-up table, we advocate for free laws of governance on a foundation of honorable moral values. We're trying to build a culture, not a gulag. Not everything is about law. Your ideas have to have merit on their own. Intellectually honest, discerning men and women can recognize that this is an issue of socially enforced policies. It's an issue of consciousness. It's an issue of culture. When it comes to raising girls into women, what landscape should we set? Even if a perfectly flat mental ground without any obstacles is desirable (and I don't think it is), it isn't possible. We must choose a slope of some kind, a general direction that we collectively encourage. That's all a culture is. Do we tilt free women toward the pursuit of motherhood and family, or do we tilt free women toward acting like the degenerate version of men? Do we encourage women to pursue areas they hate, like corporations and politics, or do we encourage them to embrace their compassionate, caring nature as mothers? I've made my position clear: I want a culture that encourages women to embrace their femininity and prioritize the pursuit of family. I want a culture that encourages women to pursue motherhood and ignore corporations while providing the freedom that allows them to make that choice for themselves.

For such a deal to be made possible, men need to hold up their end of the bargain. It's not fair to ask women to rely on unreliable men. An indulgent special-boy with his porn, nachos, and video games has no right to criticize the disastrous tenets of feminism. His actions caused the damn problem. Men need to step up and be strong, capable, and reliable. If you think I've been unfairly critical of women this chapter and would like me to go into detail about how men should do better, no problem, see chapters 1 through 9. Be better Jimmy, be better.

In hindsight, a selfish resolution is the lynchpin that has kept the egalitarian rickshaw together; feminist women are so locked into the equity perspective that they don't even hear it in their own language. It's the "for you" part of the worldview that's instigating the conflict. Doing what's best for the family is a different thing than doing what's best for an individual bank account. By creating a culture that encourages disassociation from the family unit, the feminist doctrine leverages envy, greed, and anger at a lack of individual equity to atomize people in a way that would make Big Brother proud. Ain't no fury like a woman scorned. Even altruistic moderates like my friend accept this credo of feminist equality as an ethical truth, because they don't see the harm that it does. They're moral in their heart but misled in their mind.[54] Flipped upside down, their perspective of freedom and slavery is exactly opposite to reality: modern women are convinced that a career is the source of freedom and a family is a source of shackles. They help fabricate a corporation that hates them as a debt slave instead of cultivating a family that loves them as a fulfilled, free woman. Their instincts tell them that empowerment is proportional to money because there's no power in relying on an unreliable man.

Men failed women.

Fixing our society's shattered family unit is a multilayered problem that requires men to do better as a start. A judicious man doesn't point at women and complain that they're somehow the sole cause of this giant pile of shit we call a culture. Women aren't the cause of the problem at all! They're just reacting to it. Without resources and a safe environment (which has been the job of men

---

[54]   I mean this in the least patronizing way possible.

to provide for eternity) the whole thing degenerates into morally bankrupt chaos. Creating the strongest family unit requires two halves: the man and the woman. Robust fences and sympathetic hugs. It's what we're adapted to as human beings. Men need to be stronger, more capable leaders to provide women with a reasonable opportunity to trust their instincts and commit to prioritizing for the family. As a unit unto itself, the family is a whole much greater than the sum of its parts. Understanding this perspective is the key to unlocking a woman's willingness to abandon the corporate life, instead of her children. It's a hell of a problem, but we can fix it. Just have some faith.

> You wanna know what wealth is? It's family.

Episode #855, 1:11:10

> It's not easy to communicate with people that want to be angry.
>
> True value has no price.
>
> The price of an ethical life is not fucking easy.

Episode #266

The spell of wage equality is this: back in the day, there was no wage gap because a man's income was also a woman's income.

Episode #877, 24:55

Most men want to provide for their family and they want a clean conscious when they go to sleep.

Episode #715

Women want you to lead them the out of Hell . . . Women don't want to be little cubicle tax donkeys and have abortions . . . They hate it.

Episode #687

What's your reason? Because the thing about reason, is there has to be a reason.

Episode #292

Comedy is a half-step off virtue.

Episode #225

See, sometimes to show people the truth, you have to play the buffoon.

Episode #766

You always protect that which you love.

Episode #272

Human feces is now covering the city [of San Francisco] and they're giving free heroin to homeless people, but they banned crazy straws, so yeah, I'm pretty sure we might want to start reading the Bible again guys.

Episode #289

Feel grateful that you can even feel bad, because that means you're still alive. That means you didn't sell your soul. That means you're still in the test.

Episode #724

If you're the center of the world, you're only going to wither and die. You're only going to disappoint yourself. You're only going to make mistakes. The tastes will only start getting blander, the colors will only get dimmer. But when [you have kids], you're free . . . You're free when you're not the center of your universe.

Episode #288

The point of psychology is to alleviate guilt when you know you've done something wrong.

Episode #662

Everything that people sell out for, they took from me, which is so interesting because that wasn't the important thing.

Episode #753 (bonus)

The only woman I care about if she's attracted to me is my wife. Everyone else can go fuck themselves.

Episode #644

Today's abortion is tomorrow's slavery.

Episode #276

Some women don't know the regret they will feel from abortion, when they hear the fucking skull crack and they suck it out and their maternal instincts kick in. That's devastating.

Episode #227

I don't care what other people do. My world doesn't have abortion in it.

Episode #820, 1:15:36

[Don't cave] to nonsense. When you hold that line, you get the wisdom of it. And then you realize how weak they all are.

Episode #755

I'm not defined by what I hate, it's what I love.

You don't have to be like a caricature of a warrior monster. Just. Be. A. Man.

Episode #732 (bonus)

Good God am I fucking disappointed in men.

Episode #767

The world needs men. Don't disappear.

There is nothing better than family. Nothing.

More family quotes:

The way out is right at home.

What you love, you will see everything through.

I see [God] in kids, and I see the Devil in people that want to hurt kids. It's as clear as fucking day.

Episode #300

Real work is having kids.

Episode #298

I could have lived my whole life without knowing what love is.

If there's a traffic jam [on my street] it's because someone is teaching their kid how to ride a bike.

Episode #647

Any man that doesn't plant trees for people to enjoy after they're dead isn't a man.

Episode #530

I just want a safe and prosperous family.

Love does not make you weak.

I chose life. I chose community, stability, something that you can grow in. It's cultivating.

The natural law will never change.

The past is the future.

The nuclear family is the real nuclear power.

Show [your wife] a world where she can't imagine living without you.

Episode #676

We're going to die. We are mortal. We are sand . . . This is temporary. All we have is what we pass onto our kids. We keep them safe, we teach them, we make them moral, we give them the ability to survive in one of the most hostile tragedies you can imagine, called life. If you allow people to abuse children and to make this okay, you're gone.

Episode #291

That's why planned parenthood is so devastating. Because women don't have to look into the eyes of the child they're killing. And that's one reason why it's so effective. Women would have an incredibly hard time . . . killing their babies once they've actually given birth.

Episode #299

Oh yeah, and by the way, when I was in better shape in Hollywood, I had dead eyes.

Never comply to nonsense, ever. It's the difference between the existence of an abortion clinic, and making you abort your baby.

Episode #793

My interest is in growing things. It's not in killing things.

Episode #781

Being a father is the honor of my life.

Episode #804, 1:58:07

I'm not trying to beat down on men that are having a hard time starting a family. I know that this society is not conducive to it. You have to be stronger. You have to go the extra mile. Really start something. Start a community thing. You have to do enough stuff to make a woman be like, "I want him to be my husband." That's

241

what built the world. You look around at all these beautiful cathedrals and all these parks and these inventions and stuff, those were all dudes trying to earn a wife.

Episode #857, 35:10

People with families will never be for abortions. Once you've held your baby, if you're for abortion, you're literally a fucking psychopath. The only time I was ever for abortion was when I literally had never held a baby. I didn't understand what it was . . . family is something to live and die for. Community. Family. Faith. If you put your faith in a higher court, they're bullshit you see as something to manage. Something to deal with. You deal with the laws of man and you honor the laws of God.

If you're emotionally, spiritually, and sexually detached from your wife, because you want money, you have abandoned your woman, and you won't admit it 'cause you have a piece of paper. You fucking coward.

La Leche became a mockery of itself.

Episode #239

[The wage gap] is a statistical trick to make women leave the home.

Episode #747 (bonus)

Being a father, I lost my mind but I found my soul.

Episode #288

I can tell I'm doing the right thing because my family is really healthy.

Episode #235

Have it so women want to carry your baby, where it's unimaginable for them to kill your seed because your seed is so virile and true and strong.

Episode #793

Family is strength. So many baby boomers convinced their kids that their kids were burdens. I was convinced by my father that I was a burden, and that without me he could have become dean at a better university . . . Not only am I not a burden . . . your children are your wealth.

Episode #810, 36:35

CHAPTER 11

Value of Faith

Although I've cultivated a bounty of knowledge in terms of how to think and how to live by listening to Big Bear's streams, reading books, and thinking for myself, I don't pretend to have all the answers to the questions of life. However, when it comes to the transcendent values of faith, religion, and God, I *really* don't have all the answers. When I was in high school, I was a big fan of the new atheists, guys like Dawkins, Hitchens, and Harris. In hindsight, it's not a surprise that I turned out to be a depressed, indulgent, religion-hating miscreant for a time. The empty, nihilistic philosophy of atheism isn't exactly compelling. Luckily for me, it also didn't last.

For the sake of transparency, I should quickly mention that I'm approaching the value of Faith from the perspective of a Christian belief system.[55] I'm operating on the assumption that good and evil fundamentally exist, that there is such a thing as one greater, overall, objective truth, and that the moral system of God's law is the system to strive for. My attempt to discuss Faith as follows is an attempt to more closely abide by these Christian tenets of good versus evil, comprehensive truth, and God's moral law. It is not to reinvent words in a way that would then allow me to reinvent my own morality. The equations that I introduce are simply a consequence of my engineering background and the way that I happen to think about things. They're not intended to be strict or comprehensive definitions, but rather simple, helpful tools to consider and either incorporate or reject in the much greater ongoing discussion about faith. In addition, since I'm new to Christianity and therefore likely to make mistakes, I humbly ask that you permit me any errors as I learn. How this admission of ignorance affects your

---

[55]   Faith is sometimes capitalized intentionally in this chapter for reasons that will become clear.

perspective of my analysis of the value of Faith I leave to your discretion.

So, we press on. Since I come from a background of atheism, that's where I'll begin. Atheism is a simple philosophy; it literally means "non-theistic" or sometimes, "anti-theistic". Good enough, let's pack it in. Time to go home, right? Not quite. Like a tacky late-night infomercial, there's more! Atheism claims that a discerned pursuit of knowledge must be based on facts and evidence alone, insisting that any godly philosophy is at best naive, and at worst actively damaging to the well-being of people. Casual atheists believe in Science.[56] Serious atheists detest such a statement, claiming that they don't believe in anything at all, insisting that they utilize their thinking to create Science rather than the other way around. As we'll see, atheism is a worldview built on sand. One of the great ironies of atheism is how inherently undiscerning and self-defeating it is. (*How dare you.*) In order to understand the problems with atheism, we must also understand the opposition that it's defined by: theism. We must deal with the divine, survey the sacred, and meditate beyond the material. The awkward question "Are you a theist?" can be better phrased as "Do you have Faith in God?" To get a discussion about such a question started requires either defining Faith or defining God. Let's, uh . . . go with the former.

---

[56]   Again, the capitalization is intentional.

At the risk of creating some confusion, I'm going to introduce an equation that upgrades "faith" to capital-F "Faith." To be clear, I'm not trying to denigrate the idea of faith, I'm trying to hold people to a higher standard. Too many people think of faith as some flippant thing they can just casually claim to have. It's unacceptable to me, so I'm vocalizing a more rigorous requirement: action. In order to qualify as someone with capital F-Faith, you must believe in something so completely that you act on it. This concept can be represented with an equation: Faith = belief × action.[57] This idea is echoed in the Christian Bible: "But someone will say, 'You have faith and I have works.' Show me your faith apart from your works, and I will show you my faith by my works" (James 2:18). When it comes to strong Faith, belief alone is not enough. True Faith is holding a belief so strongly that you also act upon it.

In further pursuit of understanding Faith, we now need to consider where beliefs come from. Why do we believe one thing and not another? The atheist claims to "think" their way through everything, impartially comparing competing ideas, maintaining pure reason. This is a delusion. We aren't perfect logic machines that think things. We're human beings with biases, emotional

---

[57] Henceforth, anytime I refer to Faith, I'm referring to this equation and never to the colloquial definition of faith, which seems to loosely translate to "unshakable trust" or "strong belief", depending on who you ask.

baggage, and limitations that believe them. Whether you acknowledge it or not, the world is too complex for any of us to logically derive it all. There will always be plenty of uncertainty baked into the cake. Even highly reasoned ideas are not pure logic, as the serious atheist ~~thinks~~ believes. As cooperative, tribal folk, it's just more practical to build beliefs on trusted assumptions. It's faster to assume and act than it is to spend forever pontificating about useless esoteric nonsense. And that's okay, because speed is glorious. Certain patterns just work; at the end of the day, a bit of pragmatism is a good thing. As divinely limited, spark-wielding creatures, it makes sense that we form our beliefs through both trust and discernment. It's unavoidable. We build our whole worldviews on layers of logic that eventually terminate at some basic, trusted assumption. Even if we make a conscientious effort to be exceptionally discerning (which I recommend), there is always a core of trust in something or someone that everything else is built around; there is always some basic, fundamental, trusting guess. Recognizing the truth of our limited discernment is in itself a kind of meta-discernment. It isn't stupid to recognize Faith for what it is like the atheists claim; it's astute to acknowledge how it genuinely works. You're given a choice: Do you choose to live in a grandiose delusion, or do you face the truth of your unavoidable limitations and recognize the corresponding reality that blind trust is an inevitable part of the human condition?

In their criticisms of theists, serious atheists claim that Faith is "just" blind trust, overlooking the Faith in their own lives. Afraid of the vulnerability of acknowledging their limited discernment, atheists insist that there is a hard line separating opinions of blind trust from opinions of discernment, claiming the latter for themselves. The irony of this crude worldview that pervades atheist chatrooms is that it's inherently undiscerning. The binary is bunk. People aren't split into these categories of perfect robotic logic machines and blindly faithful Church memes. The ingredients that cook up into beliefs are always a medley, some combination of both logical discernment and blind trust. Every. Single. Time. Even the most blindly trusting human beings have reasons for their beliefs. Similarly, even the most discerning human beings have trusted assumptions they rely on deep down. This gives us another equation: belief = blind trust $\times$ discernment.[58] With a quick substitution, now we have a more refined version of our first nerd equation: Faith = blind trust $\times$ discernment $\times$ action.[59] Every human being operates under this algorithm of Faith; this trio is inherent in everyone. You could think of it as what's in your heart, what's in your mind, and what's in your hands. How much

---

[58]   Again, we use multiplication instead of addition because everybody has a bit of both.

[59]   Faith = belief $\times$ action and belief = blind trust $\times$ discernment. Replace belief in the former with the two variables of the latter.

Faith you have in something is a combination of all three variables: what you blindly trust, what you discern, and what you act upon as a result of your beliefs. Atheists argue that theists who put their blind trust in God are inherently undiscerning. It's an invalid argument. Blind trust and discernment are independent variables; they can interact in all kinds of ways: both can be high, both can be low, or either can be anywhere in between. Despite the allegations of the atheists, having a high trust in God in no way implies low discernment. Likewise, having a low trust in God in no way implies high discernment. The irony of the atheist worldview is that it's a criticism of high trust/ low discernment thinking . . . based on a perspective that is highly trusting and low in discernment. "How dare you," says the undiscerning atheist.

When it comes to secular Faith, the atheists think that Science is the cat's pajamas. They're convinced that man should meddle with synthetic junk and that every idea is a good idea when it comes from a supposed authority. That's crazy. A cat shouldn't even be in pajamas. Why did anyone ever think that was a good call? Same reason that doctors have been known to perform lobotomies, prescribe meth, and hack away at genitals: because a guy in a lab coat said so. In the future, the things that scientists are doing today (like performing abortions or encouraging people to cover their breathing apparatus with a mask) will appear just as psychotic. For this same high trust/low discernment reason, devout atheists have a serious problem to address: Science is a disaster. (*How dare you.*)

A discerning mind can recognize the difference between the scientific method and the field of Science as it is practiced. They're two distinct categories of thing. One is a theory, the other has tangible moving parts. One is a verb, the other is a noun. The scientific method can be a good way of isolating a causal variable. Authentic experiments are great—I do them all the time. However, the field of Science itself is managed by a group of human beings. Just like socialism—a "perfect system"—it doesn't work out in practice the way it's supposed to in theory. The flawed human beings responsible for the field of Science create an algorithm which propagates into a failed enterprise. Common phrases like "they've done studies" or "scientists say" or, the granddaddy of all paradoxes, "the Science is settled," are all Faith-based claims that are heavy on the blind-trust portion of the equation. Does the typical atheist run the calculations themselves? No, they just put their blind trust, and by extension Faith, in men and women as long as they're wearing a lab-coat. Whether or not it's done consciously doesn't change the fact that it's done. Atheists, with their blind trust in capital-S Science, appoint the whole institution to a dismal category: botched religion. Scientists have been elevated to a priest class. They aren't criticized at all. They're considered the authority on all things truth. Atheists believe in the peer-review process, despite having no discernable reason to trust the peers doing the reviewing. It's all blind trust. Who's verifying the studies? Are they being honest? Who's subordinate to whom? Why? A degree? What does a sheet of paper have to do with telling the truth? Education has nothing to do with honesty. Blindly trusting the religion of Science is the status quo. It also happens to be a catastrophic meltdown of a system. With the dismal reproducibility rates of published studies, you may as well just flip a coin and save yourself the snub-nosed sophistry of the abstract. (*How dare you.*)

It should go without saying that scientists are not worthy of your blind trust. They're a group of people just as flawed as anyone else, likely much more flawed if they lack the Faith in God to hold their actions to a higher moral standard. The great failure of Science is how the peer-review process conflates quantity with quality. While the patchwork of peer-review is necessary to thread competing perspectives into a single sweeping spread, it has certain basic moral requirements to function honorably.[60] The individual human beings within the

---

[60] What's interesting about peer review is how it occurs organically. With the emerging world of talking-head influencers like Owen Benjamin, these famous influencers are now engaging in peer review without anyone asking them to do so. They instinctually look at each other's videos and ideas and provide critique. Science didn't invent the peer review process. It happens on its own, and it works great when done by honest individuals.

process require a transcendent moral code to keep them accountable. An atheist scientist isn't bound to any ethic of truth. Like a man behind the wheel, the intent behind the machine is what determines its direction. A group of cronies are just better at cronyism. A pack of wolves is just more dangerous than a lone wolf. Lacking God and a transcendent ideal, the lab geek is subordinate to the dollar. Peer review isn't a gold standard when the peers doing the reviewing are obsessed with gold. The intent behind the machine of Science isn't an ethical one. Atheists are pushed and pulled by the stick of fear and the carrot of greed. While the honest scientists managing their debts are trying their best, stuck at the bottom rungs scraping by, there's something much more sinister going on up top: a crew of crooked lab coats who take that sweet Hershey's grant money in exchange for a diabetic kiss of data manipulation. It's despicable. The frontier of Science is a disgrace. So, what was that about how "Science says chocolate is healthy"?

An honest, discerning, self-reflective human being can acknowledge that atheism is a Faith-based perspective. To be an atheist is to elevate scientists to the status of a priest class. Atheists don't question their religion of Science, because that would violate the comfortable blind-trust perspective that they've taken with it. Atheists tick each box of the Faith equation. They discern that the scientific method itself can be effective. That's fair. They blindly trust that scientists are performing the scientific method with integrity. That's a mistake. They act in accordance with their religion of Science. That's a disaster.

What fundamentally separates atheism from theism isn't that one group has Faith and the other doesn't. Everyone has Faith! We all act on our beliefs, which are built on both blind trust and discernment. We're fundamentally Faith-based! Since our minds operate on Faith, the institutions that we create and interact with function the same way. Faith-based minds create Faith-based institutions. Take away one religion and it'll just be replaced with another because the underlying human condition that creates all institutions is the same. As a religious institution, Science has attempted to remove the blind-trust element of thinking, but it fails to do so because men and women, based in Faith, are the ones running the whole thing.

The institution of Science isn't the only secular religion. So is environmentalism, veganism, and progressivism.[61] Every one of these -isms functions the same way: as a belief system that outsources the arduous responsibility of codifying a whole value system. That's worth saying again: the service that an -ism provides is that it tells people what to do, and they believe it. Pragmatically, men and women act on a set of beliefs built by their institutions so that they don't have to go through all the uncomfortable work of reinventing the wheel of values. The worshipped

---

[61]   Or conservatism, libertarianism, etc.

authorities within provide dogmas, doctrines, and scriptures for adherents to blindly trust and act upon. Each of these -*isms* also has its corresponding heresy, which usually comes in the form of any argument that dismantles it, no matter how well thought out. For example, regardless of the good news, if you tell an environmentalist that rising CO_2 levels are simply causing an increase in plant life and not destroying the planet, their heads will explode. For these devout adherents, it doesn't matter how much evidence or discernment you provide. Projection curves, where we are within the CO_2 envelope, or thought experiments about how CO_2 is not a poisonous deadly gas but a basic building block for life which itself tends towards homeostasis, don't help them detach if their discernment is subordinate to their blind trust in their religions of environmentalism and Science. We interact with these enterprises with Faith every time because, once again, Faith is the human condition, it's how we operate. Sure, the level of discernment, blind trust, and action varies from person to person, but everyone functions somewhere within this paradigm of Faith. Everyone blindly trusts something. Everyone naturally discerns. Everyone acts on their beliefs. This is always done in some combination. For some people, discernment is the primary driver in beliefs. For others, it's blind trust. Both types of people exist in every kind of religion, from Science to Christianity. We act in accordance to our flavor of Faith because we need our Faith. We need to blindly trust in something before we can take the first step to benefit from it. We need to discern to be able to better understand the world around us. We need to act on our beliefs to complete the cycle of Faith that facilitates our ability to thrive.

Think about Faith like a vector: it has both an amplitude and a direction. The total Faith a person has is analogous to its amplitude. The type of Faith a person has is analogous to its direction. The ultimate separation between an atheist and a theist is defined by both the amplitude and direction of their Faith. Faith in God and Faith in Science are vectors with endpoints that perpetually diverge as they grow, manifesting distinct paths for life. Diametrically opposed, one is a race to the top while the other is a race to the bottom. But which is which? To get a discerned sense of what's up and what's down, we must observe where these paths end and compare the two. What's the terminal difference between blind trust in God versus blind trust in Science? What's the terminal difference between discerning that God created us versus the Big Bang? What's the terminal difference between acting for the transcendence of God versus acting for the material of Science? Simple: everything.

Because of the contrasting directions of their Faith vectors, serious atheists and serious theists disagree on everything from the purpose of life to the nature of freedom. In terms of the latter, one of the criticisms that atheists launch at theists is how restrictive their godly laws are. "What's with all these repressive rules? Monogamy?

No sex until marriage? Delayed gratification? Lame!" says the modern atheist "Try her before you buy her, amirite, boys?" Such bravado makes a kind of sense. If all I am is pseudo-random atoms smashed together in the empty cosmic dark, spiraling away into infinite nothingness for eternity, I may as well fuck the maid. If I can get away with it, why not? Give it enough time and the dust from our bones will be gone.

What the lukewarm thinker doesn't understand (*how dare you*), is that indulgence and suicide are both perfectly reasonable, perfectly intelligent things to do if you get to the bottom of serious atheism—if you're an atheist with amplitude. This is why smart people are so cynical and prone to depression if they're secular thinkers. By their quick wit and powerful computation, they're capable of getting farther down the treacherous path of secularism than those with less cerebral prowess. Without a purpose to anything, an emptiness takes over the atheist and godly laws become nothing but a repressive restriction from hoggishly feeding the infinite void, rules that are nothing more than arbitrary injunctions holding you back from that sweet, sweet suck of dopamine. Or the seductive release of death. You could say that atheism has a rough way of looking at things. Theists, with Faith in God, see it all differently. Our worldview doesn't observe godly laws as restrictive. They're freeing. It's a complete 180. The perspective is flipped for its viewer's orientation. What defines your worldview? Is the purpose of sex to create children in glory to God, or is it to make a few neurotransmitters dance? Do you see the material as all there is, or do you see life as a transcendent test of your soul? In other words, are you free to sin, or are you free from sin?

A hotel owner learned a not-so-fun lesson recently about the supposed freedom of indulgence. Responding to the corohno viruth, the government crammed a band of homeless people into a park. Projecting, the empathetic hotel owner felt the pain of the homeless, seeing how packed in they were. He didn't want these poor souls to catch corunkee so, with a humanitarian heart, this proprietor of human honeycombs decided to let the nearby aphids in, giving them somewhere to be "safe."[62] He had one condition: Don't trash the place. For most people, a free room in exchange for a hint of responsible behavior sounds like a sweet-as-honey deal compared to a degenerate night buzzing under a bridge. Any predictions on how it went? Let's just say they did a little more than break the contract. They incinerated it. More piss hit the floor than a full-moon bucket party in Thailand. The homeless drug-addicted vagrants smashed, flipped, and stole whatever they could. Obviously. They had spent so much time indulging that their base, animal minds owned

---

[62]   Homeless people aren't really aphids. They're men and women with the divine spark too, but that doesn't fit the metaphor very well. Don't take it too seriously.

them. Simply not destroying a free place to live was too big of an ask. They were slaves to their sin.

"Aha!" says the atheist. "So there is a purpose to refusing indulgence: it works out poorly in the long term. No need for God to understand that. Everything is material. I'll just refuse indulgence. Easy-peasy." But is this true? Does the atheist anything-you-can-do-I-can-do-better claim stand up to scrutiny? Let's look at how they differ. Everyone serves something. The theist, with his Faith in God, serves God. The atheist, with his Faith in Science, serves himself.[63] To see if they can be equally capable is to ask the question: All else being equal, is the atheist, who serves himself, just as capable as the theist who serves God? Absolutely not. How strong can you be if all you answer to is a weak, puny, endlessly flawed being such as yourself? Not strong. Now flip the question: How strong can you be if you're serving the almighty creator? There's no limit. You can handle anything, because there's something much greater than yourself at stake. No amount of pain, no amount of strife, no amount of worldly hell can break someone with enough Faith in God. Not even the fear of death can break a resolute Christian. The evening news is enough to break a Faithful materialist. What the flustered atheist refuses to accept is that you don't get

---

[63]   You could argue serving others is somewhere in the middle. Voila! A transcendence hierarchy of service: service of God, service of others, service of self.

to have it both ways. You can't fake it. You can't build a worldview on sand and expect it to stand tall, because, all else being equal, the strength of something is defined by what it's made of. And your will is built out of your beliefs.

What happens when someone builds their beliefs on secularism and puts their Faith in Science? What can the downward path of atheism look like? What does that human being do with a little amplitude? They embrace the "freedom" to sin. They lie. They complain. They indulge. They watch porn. They take drugs. They fail to be responsible. They feel entitled and lose their gratitude. They become narcissistic, cynical, and sarcastic. They gobble synthetic garbage from the grocery store shelves. They extend their youth, infantilizing themselves at college. They can't permit pain, and they can't pass up pleasure. They become dictated by propagandized pixels on a screen. They take on crippling debt for the temporary rush of a status symbol. They submit to their worldly fears because they're addicted to the material indulgence of life. They lose courage and surrender the ability to speak plainly in exchange for money and social points. They marry the mainstream narrative, unable to handle the "how dare yous" that divorce them from independent thought. They fall in love with money and take debilitating jobs as tax donkeys for a beast system that disqualifies them as parents. They chug pills or become numb drones in the hellish matrix of video games just to shut out, shut *out,* *shut OUT,* the fucking voice of their soul that endlessly shrieks about the obvious, stark reality that *something is desperately wrong*. Even worse, they abort their babies.

It's tough to overstate how catastrophic Faith in Science is with a bit of commitment. Pick the wrong direction and some amplitude will kill you. Sixty toilsome years scrambling for dopamine and cowering from cortisol isn't a life. That's a tragedy. Nonetheless, I still haven't addressed the issue of discernment surrounding God. It's all well and good to claim that Faith in God works out better than Faith in Science, but such an argument is just an appeal to pragmatism. It only points at the truth in a be-known-by-your-fruits kind of way, which, for the dialectic types, isn't a sufficient argument, even if it's a great rule to live by. How then do we discern the existence of God? Without diving into anything esoteric, we can start with a fundamental question: How did all this get here? The competing answers provided by theism and atheism give us an indirect sense of what's most likely true. After that, you just have to guess and have some blind trust. This is where the Faith in Science extends into absurdist territory, revealing its hand. The priests of Scientism claim to understand—with certainty—the origin of all things. They make wild, sweeping guesses *before* reverse-engineering equations based on those same brash assumptions, which are then used as justification for the assumptions. Such arrogant and invalid circular logic is presented to the rest of us as undeniable fact. This specific criticism of Science sounds crazy if you know a little about

Science, but makes perfect sense if you know a lot about it. The field of Science claims to be the arbiter of truth. People comply to Science as the authority on describing the outside of our giant something, despite scientists never being able to step out to actually look. It's absurd. Science doctrine (and this is real) claims that nothing can ever be created by nothing, except for the nothing which created our something, which is why you're now something in a universe which is mostly nothing. What is this nonsense based on? A blind guess and a few equations invented afterwards to justify it. If that makes sense to you, I don't know what to say. Wearing this fashionable suit of secular belief requires twisting your mind into a Windsor knot, recklessly abandoning discernment for the progressively tightening neck tie of blind trust in the religion of Science. This priest class of scientists dubiously claim the "truth" of the Big Bang with precisely zero evidence outside of their circular logic machines. Blindly accepting their wild claims has nothing, and I mean *nothing*, to do with discernment. No one bothers to run the calculations themselves, let alone address their viciously circular arguments and absurd assumptions. They simply put their blind trust in the dishonest priest class of scientists, choosing fashion over function. The argument for God as the creator of everything makes far more sense.[64]

One of the criticisms atheists have of theists is their acknowledged embracement of blind trust, which they conflate to be the entirety of Faith. Atheists claim that blind trust is inherently bad under any circumstance, while, ironically, actively participating in its worst version: being blind to blind trust. They fearfully avoid the reality that we're Faith-based beings. What's important to understand about the blind-trust element of Faith is that it can be either be detrimental or beneficial depending on the context of its application. Blindly trusting someone who is predatory, like a televangelist who takes the Lord's name in vain to steal money from old women, is a problem. Likewise, blindly trusting the most morally bankrupt scientists who convince you of a worldview that prompts everything from dishonesty to degeneracy is also a problem. It's discernment that helps a living man

---

[64] For more rigorous arguments about the discernment surrounding God versus atheism, I defer to Immanuel Kant and the transcendental arguments. He's done some heavy lifting in his dense books, *The Critique of Pure Reason*, *The Critique of Practical Reason*, and *The Critique of Judgement*. Kant reasoned that one cannot prove God exists, but one can assume God exists through reason. The arrogant idea pushed by atheists that theists are by definition stupid, blind, or otherwise undiscerning is, in a word, wrong.

or woman overcome their instincts to blindly trust such snakes, whose soothing hiss sounds so promising.

However, blind trust isn't just a detriment. As we've discussed, it's an inevitable part of the human condition. Blind trust can have enormous benefits. For myself, although I'm mostly discernment driven, putting some Blind trust in God has proven to be phenomenal for my well-being. For others, I'm sure it's the same. Men and women who can put blind trust in God (which, again, doesn't mean they're undiscerning) can believe in God. Men and women who believe in God can act for God. Such Faith in God creates the most fulfilling, fruitful life possible, filled with gracious values like truth, gratitude, and family.

Like many values, what's inescapable about Faith is that it's a positive feedback loop—it builds on itself. Your life can perpetually elevate or it can consistently descend. You'll never be able to prove God (to borrow from Immanuel Kant) in any *a priori* or even *a posteriori* sense, but you'll also never be able to disprove Him either. What this means is that either direction of Faith will involve blind trust, whether large or small. Regardless of your discernment, at some point you're obligated to put your blind trust in Science or your blind trust in God. This is what it means to take a leap of Faith: to first put your blind trust in something such that you believe it enough to act upon it. Discernment alone isn't enough. The consequences of actions create justification for more actions, building on themselves, but all of it necessitates a starting point of blind trust somewhere. This idea that atheists put forward that a human being could possibly be purely rational is a fantasy. Pure rationality doesn't exist. It's self-refuting, illogical, and undiscerning. The atheists, suffering from the Dunning-Kruger effect,[65] are overconfident in their critique of theism for their failure to discern.

In short, the atheistic worldview is a disaster. My cataclysmic college experience started spiraling downwards before I had ever stepped foot on the campus; the descent began when I committed to traveling down the path of secular Faith in Science in high school. Clawing out of the pit I ended up in has been an odyssey of both challenge and reward for which I'm most sincerely grateful. To come back from being so nihilistic required a long series of lessons. One of the insights I've gathered by traveling so far down the atheism road is how progressively treacherous the descent is. Truly believing and acting upon Faith in Science with commitment is debilitating. However, many men and women who find themselves

---

[65] The Dunning-Kruger effect is a phenomenon that was discovered by comparing estimated competence verses actual competence. Those with low actual competence overestimate themselves because the skill underneath both estimating and doing is the same. The typical atheist is so terrible at discernment that they're dealing with unknown unknowns rather than known unknowns. They don't know what they don't know.

somewhere on the path of secularism aren't experiencing dire calamity. They lack the amplitude, and instead experience mild unfulfillment, general dissatisfaction, or a vague sense of unease. Diagnosing such a nebulous problem is challenging for its temperature. Although irksome, a lukewarm bath lacks either the frigid cold or the searing brutal heat necessary to organically inspire an enthusiastic leap out, because feeling something is defined for its contrast. The lifelong casual atheist has no sense of transcendent fulfillment to compare their mild nihilism to. It's hard to explain the profound difference. The consequences of the downward path of atheism only becomes obvious when you've traveled so far down the path that the sun disappears. This is why I encourage being an impactful person. If you really, truly, deep down believe that atheism is the right path, then commit to it! Don't be some lukewarm, milquetoast, split-the-difference pushover. What kind of person has so little respect for their beliefs that they don't act on them? It's better to make a mistake and learn from it than spend forever in a mushy purgatory of risk-averse ignorance. One way or another, you're going on an adventure. So go the distance.

Once you realize that Faith is the human condition, the perspective shifts from questioning the existence of Faith to questioning the consequences of its inevitable application. Pertinent questions pop up. Where is your blind trust placed? How committed are you to discerning as best you can? Will the actions, built out of your beliefs make you strong and righteous? It all amounts to the same thing: Whom do you serve?

It's worth saying one last time: Faith is an inevitable part of the human condition. It starts with blind trust, but doesn't finish there. Faith isn't exclusively blind like the atheists claim. Faith includes discernment. Some people arrive at their beliefs mostly through blind trust, others do so mostly through discernment. Regardless, everyone has a bit of both. The human mind naturally wants to make sense of things. Even the theists most committed to blind trust in God have logical, discerned reasons for believing in Him—even the few who resent me for saying so, seeing their blind trust as a badge of honor. Finishing the equation of Faith is the element of taking action. Without that final element, a belief doesn't qualify as Faith. What's important to understand is that the consequences of both the direction and amplitude of the vector of a man's or a woman's Faith will define the trajectory of their whole life. True strength requires God because your will is built out of your beliefs. If you're going to be a decisive, impactful human being, you have to commit to the path set forth by your value of Faith. It comes down to either floating down the lazy hedonic river or traversing the challenge of the upward hike. Do you see yourself as free to sin, or free from sin? Do you languish in the indulgence that secularism permits, or do you embrace the transcendence that metaphysics provides? Do you travel the path of Faith in Science, or do you travel the path of Faith in God? I'll give you one guess as to which one leads to the value of honor.

What do I do about depression? Pray. Do something. Be active. Depression is not the natural state of man. Depression is a sin. Despair is a sin. You're spitting at God if you're depressed. I understand, I've been depressed before. But it's wrong . . . There's no justification for depression. None.

Episode #779, 13:31

You can pray with your body and never utter a single word.

To me, religion is very literal . . . I live it. So many people don't live it. It's all completely theoretical.

Episode #820, 1:25:18.

We're all blind in certain ways.

Episode #303

If you don't have your own discernment, it's whatever people tell you.

Episode #1054, April 29, 2020

"Devout atheist—isn't that an oxymoron?" No, it isn't, you're committed to the lab coat. Whatever that lab coat says, you believe.

Episode #819, 1:20:25

They've become a godless Church.

I know how manipulated [science] is. You know more than half of scientific findings in the last few decades can't be replicated, ever? [Science] is all bullshit. You're more likely to get truth from a schizophrenic crack-addicted meth whore at a truck stop, because she's like, "Water is good." That's true.

Episode #820, 1:25:51

The difference between Christianity and science is that Hell will be on Earth.

Episode #263

You don't need scientific confirmation of your religion. Science is another religion.

I had to have blind faith, to get sight . . .
That first step has to be, I just believe . . .
Eyes to see, ears to hear. Seek and you
shall find, ask and you shall receive.

Episode #841, 1:12:45

The only constant in life is change, right?
So you're always going to be moving.
Which direction are you going to move?
You gonna move up or down? There's two
ways. Up or down.

Episode #1017, April 8, 2020

Some of the best, most empathetic people
in the world are the biggest junkies when
they don't give it up to God.

Episode #809, 1:35:15

That's the problem with [atheists]: they
don't think about their kids.

Episode #809, 2:01:31

The wage of sin is death.

Episode #753 (bonus)

When you're your own master, you'll always go down.

If your purpose is fun, your life is just slowly ending. The party is slowly just going to dwindle away and you will just enter oblivion once the music stops playing.

Episode #169

The truth is the armor of God.

Episode #662

If the answer to the problem that someone projects to you is only their products, they're lying.

Episode #752

When you do what is right, when you put your jurisdiction in God the Father, things just appear . . . It's just like a bird that sees a worm. And there's no way you can explain that to people that don't understand it . . . It has to be a leap of faith.

Episode #784, 48:27

Get God, get a baby, and shut your
fucking mouth.

Who's your master?

You have to understand the role of religion
in society. The role of religion in society is
to show people not to be afraid and give
people a group ability to connect to God.
If the government, because of the sniffles,
says you can't go to your church or your
mosque, and there's a group of people that
go anyway, in history they're called . . .
martyrs. And what do we all know about
martyrs? They inspire people . . . fear God
more than the state. That is what the role
of religion is supposed to do.

Episode #793, 0:08:42

More faith quotes

If you believe them, it shows you don't
believe God. This is all a test. That's why
Satan is allowed to roam this earth. God
could end Satan anytime he wants. Satan
is allowed here. Because it's always a test.
Do you believe the words of liars? The

273

media. You already know the media lies. You went through Russia collusion; you went through all this stuff. Are you going to believe them over God? Are you going to be afraid because of the media? You failed.

Episode #780

The *-isms* keep growing. False gods, false idols, the opposite of logos/truth.

The Bible is the base.

Episode #700

There's nothing you can do to a man who has will and faith and gratitude.

Episode #681

Pass the test, get the blessing.

We don't get to create God.

The handbook that gets you out of hell.

People think that being their own god makes them God. It doesn't.

The most dangerous devil is right about what he's saying.

Episode #266

Vengeance is mine said the Lord, humiliation is mine, said Satan.

Episode #547

God is above language.

I saw the Devil before I saw God.

God just wants you to *crush*.

They can't control you if you believe in God.

Episode #682

It's stunning what we could be.

Episode #706

I don't see what people are, I see what people can be.

Episode #702

Everybody has a master. Choose wisely.

Money can't get you out of hell.

Episode #231

You matter. What you do matters.

The irony about a lot of biblical stories is that it can make the hero or the villain depending on what your goal is.

Episode #272

When you have kids, you see God again.

Episode #276

Women stopped following men when men stopped following God.

Episode #733

I know the supreme justice is God, and there's people shaking in their boots right now, facing oblivion. Facing eternity. George Soros is not having fun.

Episode #724

Feeling blessed is so much more important than being rich.

Episode #663

We have all this wealth but we're losing our soul as a nation.

Episode #236

A man, or woman, with God, is the majority... how's that for tasty rhetoric?

Episode #719

God is very real. You just believing it, consents to it.

Episode #767

One man with God is the majority. There's people where if they put a gun in your face and you just don't appear scared, because [you say] . . . "I can't wait to meet my maker." That person with the gun will tremble and put it down. Fact! But you can't fake it, it has to be real.

Episode #826, 1:09:33

The point of reading the Bible is to find truth for yourself . . . not to beat it over other people's heads and say, "Oh, you're not a real Christian."

Episode #762 (bonus)

There's no truth in science. There's just facts.

Episode #272

I told everybody this a while ago. If you don't show people that you follow God's law more than the law of man, you will be replaced. Because churches just become DMVs at that point. And no one just goes to the DMV. No one goes with their family to sit at the DMV and pray to God. So if your church is feeble and weak in the face of a hoaxed plandemic which it's pretty obviously hoaxed at this point, uh, you know, you'll be replaced. And I'm not saying everyone in Germany is going to be Muslim, but a lot of women in Germany are attracted to that way of life because they feel safe and protected. Women like to be with men who fear God more than man.

Episode #793, 5:40

It really is a spiritual journey . . . You see all these how dare you people and you know they could come out of the pit.

Episode #800, 57:08

Doesn't matter the horror you've done, all that you have to do is admit it.

Episode #721

Science is a verb, not a noun . . . Science is to not be trusting, that's the entire point of science. Science is based on questioning every single assumption possible. 'Trust

Science' is an oxymoron . . . A scientist is any human being who's currently doing science. It's a verb, not a noun. Saying trust science, the noun, is literally contradictory in itself. It's a paradox, it makes no sense, and you have to watch about ten thousand hours of pornography to fall for it.

Episode #936 1:27:59

CHAPTER 12

Value of Honor

I've been listening to Owen Benjamin talk into a camera for years. The hundredth stream was good, but the thousandth stream was even better. After a few dozen streams, I wrote down one of his thought-provoking quotes. And then I wrote down another. And then another. A few years later, when I noticed I had a 10,000-word document saturated with powerful rhetoric, I decided a book was in order. I wrote a letter to the Big Bear, and upon his enthusiasm I was off to the races. At first it was a daunting task. How the hell do you sensibly catalogue 10,000 words of quotes? Like my own scatterbrain, I needed to organize an enormous array of anarchy into something streamlined. To my surprise, groups of quotes started emerging organically, united by their underlying themes. I figured I'd bolster this borrowed rhetoric with some dialectic, so I started writing. Like a tree, the whole thing steadily burgeoned out of control, both fractally and upwards. My words feverishly filled the pages. Without realizing it, I was impetuously turning a project of mostly quotes into a project of mostly writing. As I worked through some of the ideas in my head inspired by Owen's livestreams, a narrative started to manifest itself: the value of honor culture.

I never understood honor culture growing up. It was alien to me. As a kid in a suburban liberal neighborhood, I was taught that if you get punched in the face, you don't punch back. Instead, I was instructed to "take the high road" and tell an adult. Brought up by the tenets of my teachers, I was taught to be cooperative rather than conflictive. I was taught to be nice rather than honest. I was taught to uphold civility rather than honor.

Now I understand why: it's the culture that fit the environment. Civility culture is optimized for harmonizing a tightly packed group of people—just doing things to get along. In contrast, honor culture is a cutthroat code of self-reliance that keeps you alive, no matter the cost. They are two separate systems for prioritizing a hierarchy of values. For their distinct ideals, optimizing enough for one inevitably cannibalizes the other. Both paradigms are alive and well if you know where to look. Honor culture is never far away. Even city folk all know an estranged twice-removed uncle, or a distant family friend who personifies a caricature of an honorable man: he does great alone in the woods with just a knife but can never quite manage a civil Thanksgiving dinner to the point that it's endearing. "There goes Uncle Ricky again." You can always count on Ricky to get upset and rant about the importance of guns for self-reliance, the corruption of Wall Street, or the evil of abortion. To such a legendary archetype, the toothless tableside etiquette of sheltered city folk comes in at a distant second to upholding his honorable life-saving principles. Speaking pleasantly near a centerpiece is one thing. Saying whatever it takes to try to save an innocent life ten, twenty, or eighty years down the road is quite another.

What's important to understand about these two cultural paradigms—honor culture and civility culture—is that they're simply different systems. They're amoral, reactionary entities. Neither one is fundamentally good or bad, they're just algorithms of group consciousness that respond to specific environments. As systems, they affect the human experience differently depending upon the medium that crafts them—either one can get out of control if the environment prompts it to. Without discernment, it's easy for one culture to blame the other as fundamentally immoral because they rank values differently. Like the fins of a fish compared to the arms of an ape, what does well in one environment fails in another. Scale-sheathed barons of the sea can't climb trees but that doesn't mean they are wrong to exist as they are. Likewise, the assessment of different value systems depends (obviously) upon what you value. Which metrics are you using for evaluation? Scale matters. Timeframe matters. Context matters. Performance depends on perspective. But let's not fall into the trap of thinking that all perspectives are created equal. Given the human condition under God, there is a correct answer to the question of morality.

We'll start from the beginning. How did these two cultures develop? What caused the contrasting prioritization of values between honor and civility? Interestingly enough, what fundamentally separated these two cultural systems is the variable of movement. Farmers, tied to their land, started developing a culture that included the value of civility. Nomadic people, like sheepherders, maintained a culture of stark honor.[66] Most of the time, farmers would maintain an honorable responsibility of their own circumstance, but less often than nomadic peoples. If a farmer had a serious, unresolvable dispute with another farmer, he had an important decision to make: Does he resort to violence or appeal to a higher civil

---

[66] If you'd like to read more about honor culture, pick up Thomas Sowell's *Black Redneck, White Liberal.*

authority? Since going on the run or getting thrown in prison isn't a great way to provide for a family, it made sense for him to let the local governing bodies be responsible for upholding justice when absolutely necessary. The amicable reputation amongst the locals was a nice bonus too, improving both commerce and social standing alike. His civility was reciprocated by others in the town. The community was able to trust in each other and abide by the laws of their authorities, developing a successful civil existence. In contrast, by the time any authorities showed up to resolve a nomad's problem they'd find naught but dust and wind. The sheepherder could only rely on himself to do whatever was necessary to survive. His nomadic lifestyle obligated him to maintain his callous code of honor, even if it meant killing a guy for just snatching up the runt of the litter, because if small theft was not met with consequence, then no deterrent was being exercised to prevent larger theft. It's the rules of the jungle. Losing one of the sheep would mean losing all of the sheep; the herder could not allow one without being forced to endure the other. A man who lives in the medium of serious consequence and self-reliance is one who is obligated to maintain his code of honor; he doesn't have the luxury of lying to himself. His high-stakes life requires long-term logic and robust rules. While the farmer could afford to bend his code of honor and trade some of his self-reliance for more civility, the sheepherder could not.

With the industrial age has come a massive consolidation of people, swarms of citizens sticking to their concrete honeycombs. Responding to the environmental change, the culture has adapted. That's worth saying again: the culture *responds* to the environment. Close quarters encourage civil conduct. In a condensing climate, these city folk have been advocating for a progressively agreeable set of priorities. Their circumstance encourages more civility. They subconsciously learn to do anything to get along, propagating the algorithm of concurrence, like lying, ensuring others are chronically comfortable, and capitulating to social shame to maintain pleasantries. This code of civil conduct requires blindly trusting in a civil authority to maintain itself. If everyone trusts their governing institutions with a smile on their face, then everyone is best oriented to get along. They're all in the same boat, trusting the captain and rowing in the same direction. Subconsciously they know that dissident rowers make for ineffective ships. For the individuals within, the destination matters less than the cooperation. Nobody, not even someone on a pirate ship, wants to get lost at sea. Extreme Civility culture has nothing whatsoever to do with ethical behavior, strength of character, or freedom. It's about cooperation at any cost. In stark contrast, extreme honor culture seeks to rigidly maintain Faith in God, a thriving family, and self-reliant brute strength. These two paradigms of values have always been destined to butt heads, and are now culminating in a culture war for the ages.

With a little help from Hollywood, civility culture has become the normative mainstream culture for contemporary society. As far as city folk are concerned, honor culture has been effectively relegated to something about as complimentary as "country bumpkin backwoods retard." Speaking with such transparent language, however, is reserved for the deplorables. (*How dare you?*) Southern accents are assumed to belong to walking house plants, gun advocates are politically labeled as child murderers, and honest men like Owen Benjamin are accused of insanity. It's a mess. Across the board, proponents of honor culture are met with a deluge of "how dare yous" from a limp-wristed band of smarmy academics, dull SJWs, and insufferable white knights, even as their cities burn to the ground. Despite their weapons of social shame, absurd prejudice, and financial punishment aimed against honorable voices, honor culture is making a huge comeback.

Now, there's an ever-growing shift in the collective consciousness taking place. Unlike the drug-addled adolescents of recent decades, the counterculture is now speaking as the voice for honorable values. The goodness in human beings is advocating for the values of honor culture despite the absurd mainstream beatdown they receive as recompense. Men want to be strong again. Women want to be caring. The progressive movement of civility is consuming itself with fire because of the immorality it has wrought. We aren't built to be amorphous cogs in a machine; having abortions, eating junk, and taking pills so that we can be mechanical, cooperative, anesthetized little tax donkeys. The algorithm of such an inhuman system has finally cracked, passing its tipping point. The mainstream vise grip of extreme civility that has made people soft, morally bankrupt, and stupid is losing its hold. The human beings within its grasp have decided they no longer consent, changing the nature of the game from compliance to conflict.[67] As steel sharpens steel, man must sharpen man. The human beings of honor culture who are embracing the war of ideas with a growing fury are becoming sharper for it. People are done with the Devil's deal of moral bankruptcy for reprobate indulgences to get along. People are done with trusting liars and appealing to authority to be on the same sinful page. People are done with civility culture.

Here's a loaded question: Why the shift now? What prompted this anti-tolerance, anti-progressive, anti-indulgence response today and not twenty years ago? There's a prodigious list one could uncover in attempting to solve such an inquiry. One answer, however, is more fundamental. It's directly linked to the original driving force behind honor culture itself: the variable of movement.

---

[67] At this point, we're looking at intellectual, not physical conflict. Thank God.

With the emergence of the internet, information has become far more fluid. Facts flow like hot gravy: tasty yet dangerous. This medium of mobility has inevitable cultural implications. While facts are more accessible, so are falsehoods. There's no shortage of malicious liars with midget-sized blogs, or monster-sized news agencies selling you fear porn, greed porn, or porn porn. What do you do when you're flooded with misinformation and terrible advice? What do you do when you lose trust in your institutions as a result of this mobile information that, for all its flaws, also exposes lies, hypocrisy, and predators? What do you do when you realize your habits, based on the advice of those same "authorities," are actively harming you and your family? You change. You refuse alignment with the institutions claiming to be your leaders and civil moral authorities. You start thinking for yourself. You begin an honorable shift toward becoming more self-reliant. You learn to refuse the comfort of your feeding trough, becoming skeptical of the mysterious bloody hand that purports to be your buddy. Just like the sheepherders of yesteryear, modern men are learning that they must be more responsible for the care of their own mind, resource acquisition, and the protection of those they care about. Modern women are learning that they're not exactly stoked about being tricked into the sterile pen of tax chattel. Mindlessly appealing to authority is no longer perceived as an acceptable default. Now trust must be earned rather than given, and it's being earned by individuals with hearts, not institutions with harems. Instead of our previous reverence, the religion of Science now receives naught but our skepticism and rejection. Doctors don't get to cut the line anymore. "I can show you a study" means nothing. Honor culture is reemerging as the thing to do because the mobility of information is causing the turbulent environment to reveal itself as untrustworthy. We're learning to disregard the teachings of our secular, self-appointed priest class. We're recognizing that civility culture isn't the utopia that's been advertised. We're observing that the comfort of conformity comes at a cost.

With time and a large trusting population, this degenerating algorithm of civility culture has terminated at a reprobate station. In a dense population, the steep price of sheer conformity has been paid with the currency of ethics. Look around and you'll see that the seven deadly sins are rampant in cities. Ticking each box of sloth, envy, lust, greed, wrath, pride, and gluttony is about as easy as a typical Tuesday on a couch with a laptop in Manhattan.

What caused the civility culture of cities to empty the ethical coffers of its citizens, rendering the men, the women, and the institutions they constitute morally bankrupt? The reason for this moral malfeasance is simple: down is easier than up. In this game of civility culture, where it's advantageous to make everyone act the same, it's much more effective to depress rather than elevate. Hiking the hill toward strong, conscientious character is a challenge not everyone can equally manage. Languidly floating down the hedonic river of indulgence, however, is something anyone can do. For this set of civil, cooperative values, avoiding "how dare yous" is the default metric for assessing moral character. People convince themselves that they're good because they don't bother anyone. And nobody bothers anyone because they're too busy morally vacating themselves of anything worth fighting for. Instead of speaking the truth, engaging in honorable conflict, and doing whatever it takes to build a healthy family, modern men spend their time whacking off to pornos, chasing women for status, and saving the woman of their dreams . . . in a video game. The trade is pathetic. The modern wet dream is to be submerged in dopamine; to be a pickled brain in a jar in a long warehouse of isolated carbon balls that don't bother each other because they've been anesthetically numbed by their chemicals. Sinking into such compliance and harmlessness doesn't upset the modern special-boy because he likes the trade. It turns out that it's easy to enslave everybody into a dishonorable existence when it feels good. Just eat, fuck, and don't cause trouble—simple indulgent manipulation of brain chemistry to make everyone get along. It's a hell of a system.

Trained in the tenets of civility culture, the basic instinct of city folk is to avoid anything that that might cause a stir. Yelling in a supermarket is considered frightfully taboo. Justifying such an act on the grounds of violated honor is considered insane, or unhinged. Such social turbulence is breaking a cardinal rule: Thou shalt not perturb civil order. This civility-culture algorithm has gotten so out of control that the human beings within it can't even see how absurd it is. People who have literally had heart attacks in the airport (more common before the coroh-no nonsense decimated the travel economy) have claimed that the worst part of *nearly dying* was the embarrassment of slightly interrupting a few people nearby. A more extreme example (if you can believe it) took place when Owen and his mother accurately spoke out against several pedophiles in the town Owen grew up in; Big Bear and his mama were shunned by community members with "how dare yous" simply because accusing pedophiles of pedophilia happened to ruffle a few feathers of the institutions in control. Really think that through: defending children from being raped by adults is considered the wrong thing to do by the most civilized person in the room because appealing to authority supersedes the morality of honorably defending a child. Crazy. Push civility culture far enough, and such insanity becomes not the exception but the superordinate rule: cooperation at any cost. *At any cost.*

Despite such horror, it's still true that civility culture itself is just an amoral system that responds to its environment. There's nothing inherently evil about an algorithm that encourages getting along. This is where the adult conversation really starts: discerning the context that separates an amoral system from its immoral consequences because of specific conditions. It's just a robotic algorithm that gets carried away. On the reasonable end, when civility culture originated it was in the environment of a small town of honorable farmers. The cultural thing to do was to give up a modest portion of honor to get an extensive return of civility. The general vibe was about being 90 percent civil and 90 percent honorable simultaneously. Now the mainstream culture has responded to its grotesque enormity, projecting a behavior closer to 99 percent civil and 0 percent honorable onto anyone who trusts their television. This algorithm of diminishing returns—trading buckets of honor for drops of civility—has gotten exponentially out of control because the scale of the algorithm matched the scale of the environment; the population density of cities is too high and the supply chains that we engage in are too large. Even a well-intentioned, kind-hearted, civil person can't escape the destructive footprint of their actions in cities. Simply paying your taxes and getting along with enormous institutions through a bit of cordial commerce means funding everything from sweat shops and collusion to baby murder and pollution. The gargantuan civil machine has sacrificed the moral version of humanity to become the mechanical monstrosity that it is. With long supply chains, distant suffering is the cost of local comfort. You can close your eyes, tap your heels together, and repeat "capitalism saves, socialism kills"[68] all you want if it makes you feel better, but that braindead oversimplification overlooks the discernable nuance of reality.

Modern culture is completely disassociated from such an archaic adjective as "honorable." This ethical degradation has consequences. Modern men are so weak, mentally fragile, and institution-reliant that they've become morally vacant, giving up their discernment, their families, and their ethics. Brittle shells of men pushed and pulled by their the greed of indulgences and fear of discomfort. Most city boys don't even know what a potato plant looks like, let alone how to grow one. It's not hard guys—it's a potato.[69] Men have become completely unwilling to engage in even a modicum of conflict or discomfort to uphold their moral compasses. Being a pudgy, drug-addled, porn-addicted video game connoisseur is about as far from honorable as a non-predatory human being could possibly be. It's also the status quo for the lavish life of civil city boys.

All this is to say, things aren't looking great in our mainstream culture. With our enormous environment of corporatocratic, technocratic, and lie-ocratic free mobility, opportunistic predators are not being institutionally held

[68]   Shout out to MadebyJimBob for his hysterical Charlie Kirk impersonation.

[69]   Neutral pH to slightly acidic soil works best, hill up (build up dirt) around plant in the first few weeks of its growth to encourage more root (and potato) growth. Harvest when greenery dies off.

to account. At this gargantuan scale, the carrots and sticks are lined up in direct opposition to ethical institutions— if such an entity is even possible at said ludicrous size. Individual living men and women can make moral choices; a corporation, or corpus, doesn't have the beating heart necessary for such an honorable decision. There is no single living man in charge. Grow large enough and game theory simply takes over. Psychopaths aside, even good men can stomach their own contribution to something immoral because they're only partially responsible; when your responsibility is a compartment of something, it's only natural to compartmentalize your responsibility of its horror. Why—in the hell—would a large corporation optimized for economics pay for an externality when it can just pass the problem downstream?[70] Similarly, civility culture has been prompted into immorality for its scale. Such gigantic size has presented the rest of us with a titanic problem: It's too easy to be predatory and get away with it.

---

[70]   A business externality is a non-monetary cost of doing business—like pollution—that someone outside of that business has to later pay for to fix or clean up. For example, if a home cleaning product, a hygiene product, or any other synthetic garbage causes someone cancer, the hospital bill is not paid for by whichever corporate peddler sold the scented snake oil. It's too difficult to prove cause. Even if such a company knows they are causing cancer, they can, and do, simply keep quiet and sell with impunity. They're happy to kill people if doing so turns a profit.

Nothing sticks when everything moves. The delay between transgression and response to transgression is too long for any pursuing justice to be anywhere close to effective, assuming they're even trying, or that there even is a "they" who tries. For every fact check there's ten thousand new facts. And what happens when fact-checkers start lying? Or the fact-checkers of the fact-checkers start lying? Who is the authority and why? Shit is piling on faster than it can possibly be cleared out. People are drowning in it. There's no moral authority keeping the molding, putrid weight of extreme civility culture under control. Predators are everywhere, and with no competent moral institutions that can be relied upon, the appropriate response is to just check out and aim for the alternative: the values of honor culture.

What does "checking out" for honor culture look like? It means learning the skills necessary to become more self-reliant. It means refusing indulgences. It means acting in accordance with values that put family before self. It means planting trees you'll never see the shade of. It means forming communities with strong bonds. It means being willing to say no when necessary, letting the consequences be what they may. It means being honest when it would be easier to lie. It means doing the uncomfortable thing. It means refusing to take the ticket of lusty rage. It means knowing the difference between right and wrong and rejecting the nonsense of tepid academic ambivalence. It means committing to moral intent, aiming for the light, and repenting when the inevitable failure of darkness creeps in. It means maintaining strong values. It means putting down the phone, turning off the news, and rejecting the mainstream narratives outright. It means refusing to bend the knee in fear because a smarmy voice broadcast through a microphone told you to. It means thinking for yourself, using your own senses and life experience to discern, not pixels on a screen about statistics from "authorities" that you blindly trust.

Proponents of civility, however, disagree with the proponents of honorable self-reliance. They spout off all kinds of "how dare yous" if you question their intellectual jurisdiction. Leaders of civility culture believe that most people should just shut up and listen to the "experts." They believe that the unbearable, undistinguished plebeians deviating from the mainstream groupthink deserve naught but condescending dismissal. I disagree wholeheartedly. Everyone has both the right and, more importantly, the responsibility to try to discern and think for themselves in pursuit of logos. There's nothing wrong with benefiting from trusting individual men and women who have proven themselves to be consistently honest, but there is something wrong with a need to appeal to authority.

Ultimately, honor culture is about personifying strength to survive, whereas civility culture is about personifying indulgence to be compliant. It should go without saying by the way, that completely abandoning the set of principles that keeps you alive is going to create some problems. Solving this dilemma requires undergoing a major shift in perspective. It requires adjusting intent, trading civility for honor, choosing to actively defend the values that create strong families in self-reliant communities rather than the ones that create rich individuals in enormous civilizations. I've done my best to make my case on how to achieve this lofty goal clear: speak honestly, conduct discernment, embrace discomfort, manifest courage, welcome conflict, defend freedom, appreciate comedy, radiate gratitude, prioritize family, and empower Faith. And do all of it for God. Blindly trusting in the secular authority of institutions is neither virtuous nor smart. Your government is lying. Chronic comfort is a curse. Science is not God. Being an exemplar of honor isn't the ignoramus backwoods absurdity that it's portrayed on television to be, it's a sane response to an insane cultural mandate. Despite its challenge—or perhaps because of it—the honorable position to take is to be responsible for your own mind *and* your own circumstance.

Countering this perspective that I've put forward is a criticism of my position's extreme: "You can't be self-reliant for everything!" Fair enough, ghost of my culture. Although I see such a criticism as a strawman coming from a place of self-soothing and avoiding the responsibility of committing to the challenges of a more honorable life (*how dare you*), I'll nonetheless address it. At the risk of sounding like a nauseating moderate, I'm happy to advocate the idea that there's a middle ground worth aiming for, something that's both more civil than scrounging for acorns alone in the mountains and more honorable than our mainstream consumerist insanity. So what does this middle ground look like? It's an environment that organically encourages a healthy mix between honor culture and civility culture: a rural environment. A place with a population density high enough to facilitate enjoyable civil relationships with others but low enough that the families within the community are honorably responsible for the land that they occupy. Exactly how much responsible self-reliance they exercise is up to the occupants themselves. Some could use the land to grow a garden and maintain a few chickens while they work on their craft, while others may as well be Amish, doing full-time homesteading. Although such a thing is truly honorable, my argument isn't to say that every single family in the world must have a perfectly self-reliant homestead in order to be moral. I'm not arguing that specialization, craftsmanship, or commerce is inherently evil, I'm simply acknowledging the undesirable consequences of civility culture due to enormous scale.

Through a conscious choice, however, an individual can embrace the honorable values I've described in any environment. Like the manufactured-consent-versus-free-will idea discussed in chapter 7, the cultural values you choose are neither predetermined nor unaffected by the environment they're placed in. They're incentivized but not inevitable. The growth of civilization has progressively tilted men toward extreme civility and cannibalizing honorable, moral values for indulgent cooperation, but an individual willful man can always consciously choose to go the other direction, even if it's the more difficult path. Living men and women always have their free will. Subsisting in a dense urban area encourages (but does not obligate) you to be a morally bankrupt degenerate who sacrifices everything honorable in order to chronically indulge and brainlessly get along. Regardless of those carrots and sticks, you're free to get a rifle, speak your mind, and start a garden.[71]

Such thinking presents two basic options[72]: move to a rural community where the environment naturally forms a culture that's the ideal mix of honor and civility, or stay in an urban area that requires a conscientious uphill fight against puritanical civility. Which is better? That's up to you. Owen has been telling people to get out of cities for years, but he's also been telling them to bloom where they are planted. Out of context, this appears to be a contradiction, but it's not. It's an issue of discernment. As always, the circumstance matters. For some of the biggest

---

[71]   I've even seen city folk start balcony gardens and grow food inside with grow lights.

[72]   This is one of those binaries that is actually a continuum; there is an array of choices between the two extremes, but we think of the phenomenon in terms of the ends to clarify what happens in the middle.

cities, like New York, Los Angeles, or San Francisco, yeah, just get out. For the honorable man, it's important to know that conquered territory is conquered territory. If Babylon wants to fall, let it fall. For areas like the suburbs, halfway between city and rural however, it might be a mistake to flee because you think there's magic dirt somewhere that's going to solve all your problems. There are many communities that aren't as honorable as they should be, but the solution could easily be to change what you are, where you are and become a community leader in the shift towards honorable values. "Bloom where you're planted" is about pursuing a more honorable existence to improve your community despite the challenge. Maybe the move is to stay on your small parcel of land and start becoming more self-reliant. You can grow an astounding amount of food on a quarter acre. Show others what's possible. What's important to understand is that if you still hold the values of civility culture and you're planning on fleeing a reasonable area because you're scared, you're making a mistake. Best-case scenario, the cultural dissonance between you and your rural neighbors will make you miserable. Worst case, your lack of strength and self-reliance in a more challenging environment gets you killed. "Bloom where you're planted" is a call to good values despite imperfect circumstance. It implies that moving won't solve your problems if you are the source of your problems. If your choices, your lifestyle, and your values are what's causing your dilemma, then moving doesn't solve a damn thing. Being soft is a problem, but it's a worse problem if you move somewhere that requires you to be tough. If you think that being dishonest is advisable because it helps you get along with others, or that independent discernment is less important than appealing to authority, or that governing bodies should grow to give people even more comfort, or that putting on a mask is justified because a few predatory pixels made you scared, or that always choosing affable civility over honorable conflict is somehow inherently moral, or that safety is more important than freedom, or that funny jokes should be punished because they might hurt someone's feelings, or that ingratitude and sarcastic complaining is acceptable, or that abandoning the responsibility of a family for environmentalism or money is admirable, or that Faith in God is stupid, then honor culture just isn't your thing and you really should just stay where you are. In other words, if you want to bring your California to Idaho, don't bother, you'll regret it.

That being said, if you want to move to a rural place with a sensible balance between civility and honor, and you're fully assimilated to those values already, I think that's great. I'm a young man who grew up in civility culture and I could see myself moving. Being surrounded by men and women who maintain the God-given honorable values that I have Faith in sounds wonderful. For myself, I'm going to spend some time in the suburbs building gardens and see what happens; ultimately if civility-culture people want to suck on the rancid teat of government because it's easy, that's their prerogative, and I'll leave.

For some time now, I've been having trouble closing out this book. What's difficult about presenting a final message in terms of culture and values is that there are always exceptions to rules at such a large scale. Pick any virtue and I can point at its vice.

No value is a perfect value on its own; no system is a perfect system. Managed by man, these things maintain inherent flaws. We see through a glass darkly. What's enticing in the moment often fails long-term, what's tailored to an individual is not optimized for all, and what incentivizes some is a deterrent for others. Trace any demented culture back far enough and you can find a timeframe where it was reasonable for the circumstance. The paradigm of civility worked as a cultural frame for constructing economics and social order, but its effectiveness is rooted in progress, not permanence. By continually optimizing toward evermore civility, we've overshot the mark in a stupendous and cataclysmic fashion. First we obliterated the natural paradigm. Now we're shattering the synthetic one. After graduating from the food chain and completely dissociating ourselves from any semblance of God's Moral law, we're now breezing through a doctorate on phony boardroom smiles, where lying is ~~second~~ first nature. Instead of being honest and diligent seekers of what's true, civility culture takes the lazy, comfortable route, appealing to the authority of institutions and trusting deceitful leaders. Rather than raise a fuss, civil types make sure to comply to get along. Now these same men and women are militant about wearing masks, too morally vacated to discern what's going on and refuse the face diaper from big daddy government. Our culture has been optimized for civility, which is just another way of saying that it has not been optimized for humanity. Like the life cycle of an organism, our civilization has built great ungodly things on the algorithm of civil progress only to start burning them to ground when the smaller components within decide that it's time to die. In the interest of getting along to facilitate city living, the typical civil citizen simply shirks the responsibility of honorable values. They don't learn to grown or build anything. This lack of self-ownership is a problem. The easy times of modernity that has been made manifest has manufactured civil "men": weak, unethical, indulgent special-boys too busy masturbating to drug-addicted runaways on a screen to pay attention to what's going on in the real world. Obviously this isn't ideal. However, in moving away from such reprobate fragility, I don't pretend to have all the exact answers. Part of this book then, has been an exercise in subtractive epistemology: simply removing the problem rather than claiming to know the perfect solution for every circumstance. This isn't a precise how-to guide for all times, places, and things. Some principles are hard line issues (pedophilia is bad) while others are dependent on context, like the question of economic scale and community structures. Part of living honorably will mean making the conscious choice to shrink supply chains. But how much smaller should they get? How strict must this ethic be? Should a community of ten thousand be *mostly* self-sufficient or *entirely* self-sufficient?[73] I don't know. It's obviously a real challenge to craft an entire civilization that's both honorable and economically effective at the large scale for a long time. It might even be impossible. At any rate, it's above my pay grade. Nonetheless, I feel compelled to delineate my perspective about culture and advocate a general sense of direction. It comes down to this: The value of honor is something worth pursuing. Nested inside of this cultural paradigm is an entire zeitgeist about what is means to flourish as burgeoning men and women. Part of thriving means surviving. And part of surviving means avoiding not only the death of your body, but the death of your mind and the death of your soul. It is in this way that modern men and women are fighting for survival: by making every effort to speak the truth and uphold our moral compasses with all the honorable values that naturally follow. We seek to keep the spark in our eyes. To this end, I hope I've made my point clear: honorable values should supersede social shame. "How dare you" is used as leverage for control; a wretched tool that progressively twists the moral code until it's upside down. Sticking to the

---

[73]   By self-sufficient I am referring to the whole community, not necessarily every individual within that community. I'm not opposed to specialization up to a threshold.

values of honor is the way to counteract the torque and keep everything right-side up. It's how we win. Our reemerging medium of mobility via the internet has made these ideas clear. A cascade effect has begun: the movement of facts and falsehoods has incentivized choosing honor over civility. This will only grow. Blind trust in the supposed authority of Science, the news, or enormous institutions has no place in a world that's proven itself to be filled with liars. Despite the squawking of SJWs, strong men don't bend the knee and capitulate to the shrillest voice in the room. Likewise, compassionate women don't abandon their children to slake the appetites of corporate demons. In light of such dark wisdom, as honorable men and women we must act on what we believe. We are the arbiters of our own culture, where our prudence is defined for our conscientiousness. Are we willing to do the difficult thing? Are we willing to take impactful steps to create the world we want? Are we willing to form strong communities that instill the cultural values that God's grace has given to us? If the answer is yes, then what comes next is simple: With the rejection of one culture comes the need to reinforce another. It's time to build.

> There's been one movement, forever. It's just good, true, beautiful versus lie, evil, wicked.

Episode #656

If you're from certain cultures, if someone hits you, you hit them back, and you hit them harder.

Episode #749

There would be no abortions if men actually followed the laws of God.

Episode #793, 1:33:07

Every single action by evil is to break the family, break faith, break the community, break independence.

Episode #1019, April 9

You're not saved by the government. You've gotta live better . . . We need a few decades of living properly before people can even address any of the legal problems we face.

Episode #786, 33:35

Do you want to have morality or do you just want to follow the leader?

Episode #870, 1:08:44

If you think a word then say a different word, you don't get virtue from that.

Episode #86,3 32:26

Be kind to yourself . . . understand that you're just working through shit. I don't know the end truth of a lot. I don't know what the real answer is with a lot of this stuff. I just know the principles to get to good places.

Episode #289

People who promise secular utopia are always lying.

Episode #244

We have an issue of morality in this country. You saw my family. I'm crushing. Family is everything. Love your family. Love your wife. Honor your wife. Serve your wife. She serves you, she honors you. You honor God. Your children: cherish them, protect them, guide them, discipline them. That's how you [win].

Episode #769 (bonus)

Guys, listen, get mad at me if it makes you feel better. I can handle it. I'm serious . . . the amount of "how dare yous" I've shouldered in my life would blow your fucking mind. And looking back, not only were we morally right, it's insane that people were persecuting [my mother and me] for calling out the rape of children.

Episode #826 18:28

Here's the thing about government: If you want limited government guys, you gotta live limited government. You gotta live a moral life.

Episode #856, 1:55:02

Empty people get animated by evil.

Episode #754

People will do what they're told as long as they can pass their problems downstream. We're watching this on a global scale right now.

No one is here to save us guys, we're on our own. I don't care at all about the political process. This is just the rantings of a falling empire, and I just want out.

Episode #677

You don't have to believe and follow what awful people say.

People who say the American dream is done are lazy.

Episode #677

You can always live simpler. You can't get your ethics back.

Episode #294

Bloom where you're planted.

So many people are trying to get back to a world they couldn't survive in.

Episode #713

Over time you start realizing the absolute strength of shared ethics, shared morality, and shared standard of life, . . . you go to family, church, community, then government. If we don't see that, if we don't turn that around, what's coming is centralized government. Centralized control of our lives.

Episode #239

Now do you realize your problems have always been your own?

Episode #810 19:28

More honor quotes:

Morality is the whole fucking war, guys. If you think you've lost, if you think the world is over, it is for you . . . You only lose when you agree to lose.

Episode #723

It's not the hero's journey anymore. It's the victim's squabble.

Episode #251

You can't make deals with morality.

This isn't about survival, it's about waking up to life.

I know people that were the most free in prison . . . prison has more honesty than the current structure of our society.

Episode #727

They never would have done what I did . . . my world got torched.

Episode #292

All they can do is attack my character.

Episode #636

This isn't a victim culture. This isn't a culture where if something bad happens you hold on to it and become a dickhead.

Episode #239

To stand up to the lie, you have to have low sin in your life.

Episode #661

It's the emotional reaction that keeps you blind to the big picture.

Episode #753

The way out of this is to do our own thing.

Episode #236

I represent the majority of America.

Episode #227

I believe in a bottom-up style of governance.

Episode #227

People don't see the big picture. When we kiss this place goodbye, I want my scorecard to punch out good.

When you grow fast, there's a lot of pain.

Episode #809, 2:06:48

As someone that's been moderately rich, and really poor in the same year and a half a few times in my life . . . there's nothing there. And you can get mad at me all you want . . . it doesn't do it. It just doesn't satisfy anybody at all, and it's not real wealth. Real wealth is trust. Family. Faith. Truth. Soil. Food. Health. Life . . . Security . . . money literally doesn't bring any happiness at all.

Episode #1015

Get stronger to the point where you don't give a shit.

Episode #853, 1:13:05

I think community-sufficient is almost better than self-sufficient

Episode #866, 13:43

If you take money over morality, you'll lose every time, and no one is going to save you.

Episode #677

You can't kill evil with people, you have to morally grow out of it.

Episode #753

Look at the weakest places in the country. It's all the most comfortable weather, with the most comfortable services, the most amount of . . . whatever . . . lollipops. That's what's ruining people.

There [aren't] many evil-doers. There's evil-followers.

Episode #302

The point is, most of the horror that we have to deal with as non-wicked people, comes from city living.

Episode #921 11:33

Guns are great, and scary . . . responsible gun owners are what make America run. But a criminal with a gun, you want them to have not a lot of rounds. You know what I'm saying? . . . When you're living in a honeycomb hive like New York city, the last thing you want is guns around. If you live in anywhere normal, like a natural way of life, you want every man to have at least a few guns. The more rounds they can operate the better, because that gun will protect the food from predators, it will protect the home from invaders yada yada yada. But in a city, it's like throwing a knife in a gen pop in a prison—you don't want that. That's why these arguments are so triggering to people, because they're arguing from two different points. Like a gun in downtown San Francisco is more likely than not used in a violent sex crime . . . it's scary for people. A gun in a rural environment is fundamental for protection, hunting, all kinds of stuff.

ACKNOWLEDGEMENTS

As strange as it sounds, this is one of the most unsettling parts of the book to try and write. For my earnestness, expressing my gratitude feels like an enormous responsibility. First, I'd like to thank my family. I don't know where I'd be without them—certainly nowhere good. My mother, for her endless compassion; my father, for his quiet determination; and my younger brother, for his endearing quirks. I'd also like to thank my grandparents, who have personified the archetype of altruism. Altogether, they've been the best family I could ask for. I can't remember a single time—not once ever—where I felt that I could not rely on my family. I love you all and I am eternally grateful.

To Owen Benjamin, the Big Bear, I also have much thanks. His principled stand against moral bankruptcy and his stalwart work ethic through his livestream has done much to adjust the cultural zeitgeist toward a more honorable paradigm. For the same reasons, my own personal microcosm has made a similar shift in principles; finding the values that I've outlined in this book has been in no small part due to listening to Owen's livestream over the last few years. The fact that the comedic medium through which he works is so enjoyable is just a big ol' bonus. I'd also like to express my gratitude for HandDrawnBear. She's the generous, friendly Canadian who donated her time to craft all the fantastic drawings you see in this book. Lastly, I'd like to shout out all the bears in the community that Owen is building. This conscientious, strong, and honorable group of people is the best out there. All the bears I've met, especially the ones here on Vancouver Island, are legends. Thanks to everyone for your emails, contributions, and, most importantly, just doing what you do. In this modern age, it's up to people like the bears to empower the next generation that will uphold an honorable culture.

ABOUT THE AUTHOR

With the education of an engineer, the experience of a professional athlete, and the mind of a writer, Jacob Telling is someone you might call a jack of all trades. When he isn't writing, Jacob spends his time training as a professional guide runner, designing and building urban gardens, and playing or composing music. Jacob has also been known to sell homemade woodworking projects, work as a landscaper, and design online calculators as a junior engineer in the oil and gas industry. Temperamentally, Jacob most aptly fits the Bravo male and INTJ personality archetypes. He performs best as a second-in-command for a strong leader and has a love for both understanding systems and the authentic creative process.

Jacob Telling

Check out my website or get in touch with me on Instagram. I'm looking forward to meeting more legends and writing more books.

JacobTelling.com
@RunnerBear_

HandDrawnBear

Show HandDrawnBear some love! She's a talented artist who's always producing at DLive and Instagram.

dlive.tv/HandDrawnBear
@HandDrawnBear2.0

Owen Benjamin

Of course, the Big Bear doesn't need any more introduction. If you haven't seen these websites, be sure to check them out.

Unauthorized.tv
Hugepianist.com
UnbearablesMerchandise.com,
TheGreatBearTrail.com,
BeartariaTimes.com,
BearVibe.com,
BearSaloon.com,
BuyBrosher.com.

APPENDIX: EXTRA QUOTES

"Don't shoot the messenger." No, but I understand how messengers get shot. They force it without consent . . . some people don't want to hear it.

Episode #1029, April 15

The moral of the story is a man is a fool who knows the price of everything and the value of nothing. John Wick knows the value. John Wick is a haunted man. John Wick is damned but he fell in love.

No, I don't fear death. If you're not looking forward to that eternal sleep, you're not working hard enough.

Episode #575

People have so much time on their hands they're descending into impulses.

Happiness is not the goal. Purpose. Happiness is a by-product of purpose.

Episode #508

I don't talk from a victim's standpoint, ever.

If you're honest, people are going to turn on you a lot in life.

Episode #540

My audience keeps growing even though I keep banning everybody.

IG stream 11/16/2019

The unpredictable are the scary.

Episode #283

Addictions come out when you're really, really lonely.

Episode #508

When presented with new information, you grow and you can say "never again."

One of the greatest paradoxes in the world is that you are not free until you admit you are a slave.

If you don't go to the root of the weed, it just grows back stronger.

Supporting mental illness is the worst thing you can do to people.

Self-obsession is what implodes everything.

Unlimited choices make you crazy.

You have the right to question anything you want.

When people say "how dare you," I usually just dismiss them completely. Because it's about their emptiness that they're upset about.

Episode #867

Many people are alone in groups.

I get it, I've heard a million "how dare yous."

Episode #1044 April 24

Addictions come at you when you are really lonely. Talk!

Hollywood's zip code might as well be 666.

Critical thinking terrifies people with false power.

Look at that guy . . . he just lies down on his couch he didn't make, using money that's debt, and just stuffing his face with all the animals that someone else had to kill. But yet he's the first one to point a finger at ya and say "how dare you."

Episode #815, 48:22.

Comedy a lot of times is so true it's funny. This is so true it's sad.

Episode #252

How much do you really love truth? How much do you really believe what you say you believe? And that's why I've developed this disdain for a lot of these dogmatic Churchians who think the truth is simply obeying a secular authority without any principle behind it or action or suffering at all. The suffering is actually a good thing. The more suffering you feel and can endure the stronger you will get, the more deadwood is burned, the more that which is illusionary is revealed . . . God doesn't hurt us to be cruel. It's a gift . . . As it's happening, there's nothing you can do . . . You can crack people more [with] what the internet has become, as far as shame, and these false fears, than waterboarding . . . To make it through to the other side of being tested is: how much do you really love what you say you love? Will you crack? And if you don't crack, it just becomes so peaceful.

Episode #755

I'm just damaged enough, where I had the drive to go to Los Angeles and have eyes on me . . . that comes from damage."

Episode #300

I've paid to be able to speak this truth.

Episode #702

I've had a pretty crazy year.

That might as well just be a button people push: "How dare you?"

Episode #778 (bonus)

For all my faults, I'm not a snake.

You live your whole life wondering why that big bank account never made you happy.

Episode #548

Every time you look at other people's needs, your family's needs, or the future—and suffer for it—that gets you one step away from self-absorption. And self-absorption always leads to hell.

Strip clubs are the least sexual place on [Earth].

Episode #288

I'm not here to wake people up or start a Church. I'm literally a comedian and a dad. It hit me like a fucking ton of bricks.

That's the path. The path is just do your thing right.

Episode #708

There's seven-year-olds getting castrated legally.

Episode #655

The underlying substructure of a song is the story of the chords.

Episode #226

Why live your life silent because someone else doesn't want to be offended?

Episode #254

Evil can't create. It can only mimic and mock.

Money isn't evil. Love of money is evil.

You can't buy your way into bad behavior here.

Episode #844, 20:44

Outrage shows in-rage.

Episode #810, 1:16:26

[Blues] is about the raw honesty of the human condition.

Episode #224

Takes a village to raise a child, but it takes a child to raze a village.

It's a wakeup call that you are below the people you look down on.

Episode #640

When your brain shuts off, you can then feel the freedom of psychosis.

People create a reflection of what they are inside.

I knew from an early age that at any point life could be taken from me and so I couldn't get too attached to it.

Ignorance is bliss but if anything happens you die.

Give them so much rope they can't hang you.

Sometimes the major chords are sadder than the minor ones.

Sorrow helps you understand.

Success shows them their failure.

Caring is what life is.

It's just how people who aren't short speak.

You can't predict what weak people will do.

When you see what hurts people you see who they really are.

The villain doesn't think he's the villain.

You can't brush off the monsters and say they're not one of you.

[Constantly washing your hands is] your subconscious responding to poisoning yourself all the time.

Episode #786

The last thing I want [my children] to have is a worldview that's created by [a] base reality of lies . . . and [I'll] be taken out of context. That'll be in my Wikipedia . . . it's over. They're chasing after a horse that's out of a barn saying "close the barn doors!" Everyone's sick of it.

Episode #747 (bonus)

So much evil in this world is done because people say "we" instead of "me."

Episode #743, 58:58

Organizations can only do what the people that are part of it are.

Episode #751

You can't be condescending and give no information simultaneously.

Episode #294

Sometimes you can die on the high ground

Episode #271

I figured out today I've done [2100] hours of streaming ... Always, always, always be weary of my quotes and hit-piece videos. If you can't make someone look crazy with [2100] hours of them talking off the cuff into a webcam, then you're stupid.

Episode #694

You learn so much more about what other people believe by how they view you than anything else.

Episode #276

Happiness is indicative of purpose.

Growth is offensive

Episode #283

[Suicide] is a punishment for those that loved you, and what is more cruel than that?.. ... The people that took the risk of loving you are punished for that. And you could get out of the depression . . . There's no point where you can't return . . . You don't know . . . The amount of death. Pointless nihilist, atheistic death that's happening in America right now—and I'm sure in other parts of the world—is mind blowing. And it's people who could thrive . . . [Hard work] will pull people out of nihilism faster than any rehab . . . money won't save you. It won't. It will not. Money can help you; it won't save you. It won't get you out of the darkness . . . When I condemn suicide it's not to spit on the graves of the dead to disrespect them. It's to spit on the grave of [the next] person and disrespect him so that people know it won't be an easy death for them if they want to take their life, and the more people that join me in the condemnation of suicide, the harder it is for people to kill themselves. 'Cause even in the darkest chambers of the hell of depression, the fact that you know that people will spit on your grave makes it harder. And just that little bit of resistance could save your fucking life. And so, all the people telling me I'm human garbage, and that I'm just a mess, and the fact I said that makes me evil, I don't give a shit. I know that what I said could save lives . . . Suicide is a cowardly act.

Episode #266

You can't be rock stars and Coca-Cola.

Episode #278

Once you're given the mic for real, people get weird.

Episode #271

People project what they are onto others.

Episode #266

My natural state is thinking.

Episode #266

Don't get too excited in the good times, and don't get too sad in the bad times.

Episode #694

You can't live like you're expecting to win the lottery.

Episode #281

They only get privileges if they act like victims.

Episode #687

It all breaks down to blood and lead and death. That's it.

Episode #687

The worship of [logos] is in the music. It's all perfect logical music.

As soon as you stop seeing reality for what it is, that's on you, man, and don't say I didn't warn you.

Episode #663

The price of sin is that you don't get to see anything.

Episode #667

Sometimes it can be harder to see it when you're in it.

Episode #667

I refuse to follow the rules because . . . I know I'm not a racist.

Episode #251

One individual can't restructure society and make it better.

Episode #254

Cowards don't even get the satisfaction of going to hell.

Episode #261

[Vox Day] made a great point that I don't agree with, which I find very valuable.

Episode #260

[So many people] don't understand how easy it is to buy a man.

Episode #674

Cut your grass if you're sad.

Episode #261

We're the majority, we just have no airtime.

Episode #262

The comedian exposes the fraud.

Episode #677

Caring for others will break your ego.

IG stream, 11/16/2019

Yeah, well, when the building is on fire, you react differently than it it's not on fire.

Episode #226

I don't think there's anything wrong with wealth, but it isn't something that someone can use to [leverage] me.

Episode #225

Money can start operating like a golden prison.

A good guy doesn't have a vault of gold.

If your desire is money, you're already dead.

There's nothing they can take from me; there's nothing they can give to me.

I think people fight wars not over what they hate, but what they love and what they're trying to protect.

Episode #225

All generalizations are false.

[September 27, 2017] is the day it all changed.

Episode #226

We're in a stadium right now and people can't even see it.

Episode #239

Some people are very smart and they just don't know it.

Episode #695

My personality was formed in a time when you are held accountable for what you say.

Episode #684

This is so new there's no horror in it yet.

Episode #286

If a child has the authority to choose their gender, they have the authority of choosing who they have sex with.

Episode #765

There's a difference between people that want to support me and people that want to be me. I'm always wary of people that want to be me.

Episode #701

Heroes get broken by establishments.

Episode #290

Men with influence are like hot girls. I just don't want to be used.

Episode #702

We have international currency, and that currency is skills.

Episode #292

Art can't die. It's like killing God. It's not possible.

Episode #704

I'm thirty-nine and I've lived like eight lifetimes at this point.

Episode #705

I'm so happy that I get pissed off against people that threaten it.

Episode #299

When you're in motion, life becomes more visceral.

Episode #300

I want to be around human beings that talk with tone.

Episode #711

It's an interesting time to be static.

Episode #301

When the Devil offers all of the land to Jesus, it wasn't his to give.

Episode #719

You can live your life any way you want if you have enough will.

Episode #734

The fact that I don't have a mask isn't a bad thing.

Episode #730

Looking back, I don't think I could have not drank alcohol in LA. I had no idea it was a coping mechanism.

Episode #727

It's so obvious that it's lies that people are trying to make you do. And if you bend to shame and not truth, you get just engulfed. And you have to be able to not do it just for the sake of it . . . The whole tactic is the same as child abuse. Shame. Make people feel small. Threaten that their parents won't love them . . .

Episode #755

The moral transgress isn't in the person forced to be in tyranny.

Episode #754

What does that do? To just constantly make the internet, like, the biggest campfire ghost story in history.

Episode #754

It's so much work to be lazy.

Episode #234

You can't think about existentialism when you're changing a diaper, you know what I mean? It just is what it is.

Episode #294

Real intelligence is whittling something down so you can explain it to a child.

Episode #300

If people don't change and grow, you're watching a frozen man.

Episode #721

Don't have a price.